THE GOVERNMENT AND
CONTROL OF LIBRARIES

THE GOVERNMENT
AND CONTROL
OF LIBRARIES

K. A. Stockham

A Grafton Book
ANDRE DEUTSCH

FIRST PUBLISHED 1968 BY
ANDRE DEUTSCH LIMITED
105 GREAT RUSSELL STREET
LONDON WC1
COPYRIGHT © 1968 BY K. A. STOCKHAM
ALL RIGHTS RESERVED
PRINTED IN GREAT BRITAIN BY
TONBRIDGE PRINTERS LTD
TONBRIDGE KENT
SBN 233 960236

FOR JEAN

Contents

The Government of Libraries

The ultimate responsibility for the policy, efficiency and
management of a library does not lie with the chief librarian.
Whatever the type of library there can hardly be found a
case in which the librarian is in complete control. Almost
without exception the librarian is the servant of a higher
authority; he may be very powerful, with immense freedom,
but he acts as a professional executive who exercises his
skill and expertise as the employee of a governing body.
Indeed only a few libraries, such as the London Library,
exist nowadays as institutions in their own right. Even the
national library of the British Isles, the British Museum
Library, is but one part of a larger institution, the British
Museum.

It is the governing body of an institution which has the
overall responsibility for its library service, and this body is
always the holder of the purse strings. Whichever body
controls the financial support given to the library has the
ultimate authority over it. Librarians control but they do not
govern. Later chapters of this book are concerned with the
control of libraries, but first it is necessary to examine in
detail the government of libraries.

The central government of the United Kingdom has a very
large responsibility for the country's libraries. The Depart-

mental Libraries of the Board of Trade, the Foreign Office, and of the other Ministries, are entirely its concern, especially their administrative and financial control. A great many other libraries, such as those found in universities, schools, colleges, and in local authorities, i.e. public libraries, are dependent on it to some extent for finance, especially as they are controlled by it through audit checks on expenditure or through inspection.

NATIONAL LIBRARIES

The financial support for a national library always derives from the central government of the country. The British Museum is the national library of the United Kingdom, though Scotland, Wales and Ireland also have national libraries. The administrative expenses of the entire British Museum were estimated at £2,080,000 in 1966–67 and were met by a vote under 'Museums, Galleries and the Arts', Class VIII of the Civil Estimates. The Government is not directly concerned with its administration, and for its control it appoints a Board of Trustees, composed of twenty-five eminent citizens representative of the nation's scholars as follows: (a) one nominated by the Sovereign on the recommendation of the Prime Minister; (b) fifteen appointed by the Prime Minister; (c) four appointed by the Treasury on the nomination of the Royal Society, the Royal Academy, the British Academy and the Society of Antiquaries of London; (d) five additional eminent persons nominated by the Trustees themselves.

The National Library of Scotland is governed by a Board of Trustees which is composed of representatives of the Faculty of Advocates, the universities, local authorities, Crown trustees and ex officio members, while the Court of Governors which is responsible for the National Library of

Wales has a remarkable composition – a President, Vice-President, Treasurer, and representatives of the Privy Council, universities, colleges, local authorities, Lords Lieutenant and Sheriffs, major benefactors, the thirty-six Welsh Members of Parliament and twenty-one co-opted members. Its executive body is the Council which is in effect a sub-committee of the Court.

Other institutions which may be considered to rank as national libraries are the National Reference Library of Science and Invention (formerly the Patent Office Library) and the libraries of the British Museum (Natural History), the Science Museum and the Victoria and Albert Museum. The British Museum (Natural History) Library has its own Board of Trustees, much smaller in numbers than for the British Museum. On April 1st, 1966, the Patent Office library was transferred to the Trustees of the British Museum and renamed. Although it has a separate advisory committee independent of these trustees, the NRLSI now forms a part of the Department of Printed Books. As the Science Museum and the Victoria and Albert Museum come under the Department of Education and Science, they are in effect governed by Parliament to whom the Minister responsible for the Department is answerable.

Although the National Central Library and the National Lending Library for Science and Technology carry the word 'national' in their titles, they differ radically from the ones already mentioned, an essential characteristic of which is that they are great collections for reference use only and do not lend their stock. Nevertheless, this may be the place to mention that the National Central Library, a chartered body, is controlled by its own Board of Trustees, mainly composed of public figures, and an executive committee, mostly librarians and other representatives of the principal users, namely the contributories to the Library, Aslib and the Regional Library systems. It is the pivot of the inter-library lending scheme in England and Wales.

In complete contrast, the National Lending Library for Science and Technology is a special lending library provided through a Government department. Established in 1957 as part of the Department of Scientific and Industrial Research, it is now a section of the Department of Education and Science and is controlled by a Secretary of State responsible to Parliament. Though it has a committee, this is only for consultative purposes.

ACADEMIC LIBRARIES

(a) UNIVERSITY LIBRARIES

The cost of the majority of university education today is met by the central government. It raises the money through a vote on the Department of Education and Science on the advice of the University Grants Committee, which allocates its funds in quinquennial cycles.

A university is granted a Royal Charter determining the constitution of the governing body, usually known as the Senate or Court, which endeavours to be representative of local interests within the area over which the activities of the institution extend, and which by reason of its resulting size, is bound to delegate executive functions to a more manageable body, the Council. This, like the Senate, is composed mainly of representatives drawn from the same area, but fewer in number. The academic staff is represented on both bodies. The Council manages the whole of the revenue and as it is in effect the controlling body of all but purely academic activities, it carries overall responsibility for the library provision in the university.

In all universities, responsibility for the library, its

maintenance and development, the making of regulations governing its use, as well as the making of recommendations on its finances, is vested in a committee, usually a Senate committee although in a few universities it is a joint committee of Senate and Council. It may be composed of representatives of the faculties (and often appointed by them) with the Vice-Chancellor, his deputy and some other officer of the university – such as the bursar, treasurer, registrar or secretary attending as *ex officio* members. The Vice-Chancellor is usually the chairman. The day to day work of a university library is administered by a librarian who is the principal executive officer, and in England is usually of professorial rank and a member of the University Senate which determines policy in academic matters. Whereas most librarians act as advisers to their committees, the university librarian should be a member of the committee itself; usually in practice either he or the registrar acts as secretary to it as well.

In complete contrast and quite different is the University of Oxford, which is a self-governing corporation. Its principal library, the Bodleian, is managed under the authority of a committee called a Board of Curators, which numbers nineteen, namely, the Vice-Chancellor, the Proctors and the Assessor, seven members of Congregation (which is composed of Masters of Arts actively engaged in university work) elected by that House, six members of the Congregation elected by the Professors of the various faculties, which for this purpose are divided into three groups, and two members of Congregation elected by Council, one of whom must be a Curator of the Chest, the body responsible for financial administration. The curators are entrusted with the general control of the affairs of the library, including the appointment of a librarian, subject to the approval of Convention, and are responsible for the expenditure of all money accruing to them through the University Chest or otherwise. They must submit their accounts annually to the University Auditor, and lay before Congregation a printed report on the state of the library and its finances.

Oxford has, of course, many more university and college libraries which all follow the general pattern of control by library committees (with a variety of names) and are financed by a bewildering variety of methods, but always basically from State funds.

(b) EDUCATION LIBRARIES

This group covers a very wide field and includes Colleges of Education, Colleges of Further Education, Technical Colleges, Colleges of Art, Agriculture, Mining etc., and all the state primary and secondary schools. In England and Wales, the state school system is highly decentralized, education being the responsibility of local education authorities, mainly the administrative counties and county boroughs. The Department of Education and Science controls the whole system mainly through the scheme of inspection and with power derived from statute, and local education authorities receive detailed suggestions through circulars and administrative memoranda. The expenditure of local education authorities is met partly from rates and partly from central government grants.

It is therefore clear that the central government exerts great influence on the government of the libraries in all educational libraries.

In the Colleges the librarian (or tutor-librarian) is usually directly responsible to the principal, who is in turn responsible to a Board of Governors and the local education authority. He may attend meetings of heads of departments or boards of studies, thus ensuring that his library is able to play an indispensable part in college developments and activities. Some of the larger colleges have library advisory committees which are mainly concerned with formulating a sound library policy and which assist the librarian, who usually serves as secretary, in formulating proposals to the governing body.

The managers or governors of a state primary or secondary school are responsible for ensuring that it is managed in line with the policy determined by the local education authority. It is this latter body which bears the responsibility for the quality of the library provision. The head teacher carries out this policy and in nearly all schools he gives charge of the library to one of his teachers. Only a handful of secondary schools at present employ a chartered librarian but this situation is likely to alter considerably with the development of comprehensive education.

In matters of educational policy local education authorities are by no means their own masters. Her Majesty's Inspectors of Education are employed to visit all state educational institutions, to inspect them and to furnish reports. As library facilities may be commented on in their reports and since their contents are made known to staff, managers and the members of the education committee, they clearly exert influence and control on all state education service libraries.

SPECIAL LIBRARIES

(a) GOVERNMENT DEPARTMENTAL LIBRARIES

It is not easy to generalise about the organisation of departmental libraries. In some cases the controlling officer is the establishment officer or director, but in others the controlling body may be the Information Directorate (e.g. the Ministries of Agriculture and Health), the Technical Directorate, and

B

in Ministries with a long tradition such as the Common-
wealth Office, the controlling authority is the Assistant
Under-Secretary of State.

As the library is a common service to a whole department
with the librarian responsible to a specific controlling officer,
the creation of a supervisory committee is not widely
practised. The Treasury considers that committees are not
essential to the running of Government libraries. In a few
departments there are library committees meeting possibly
about three times a year; sometimes a committee is created
solely to determine library action in relation to new lines of
policy. In research establishments, where the librarian works
in close collaboration with the scientific staff, a library
committee is considered to be unnecessary. Nevertheless
some of the larger establishments with a main library and a
number of divisional libraries, e.g. the Royal Aircraft
Establishment, maintain a committee to ensure satisfactory
liaison.

All expenditure on books, periodicals, newspapers and
official publications is met out of funds voted annually by
Parliament for HMSO use; it is not met out of the specific
departmental vote. As a Government library uses Stationery
Office money, all its purchases remain the property of
HMSO and are stamped *For public service*. Each year HMSO
allocates its book vote for departmental use and it is frequently
the Government Department librarian who has the delegated
responsibility for administering this allocation for books and
other publications.

(b) LIBRARIES OF LEARNED AND PROFESSIONAL SOCIETIES

Since the funds for the provision of a library service are
derived from members' subscriptions, it is customary for the
librarian to be responsible for the administration of the

library through a library committee. The committee in turn is responsible to the Council of the society, an elected body taken from the membership. Like public library committees, these library committees used to have considerable powers in the administration of the library, dealing with staff appointments, book selection and library routines, but nowadays the librarian is normally responsible to the chief executive officer, i.e. the Secretary, for day to day affairs and to a library committee for policy decisions. Thus the library committee represents the interests of members and is mainly advisory.

(c) INDUSTRIAL LIBRARIES

(i) *Industrial firms*
The decision to provide a library and information staff in an industrial firm will be taken at management level and is recognition of the fact that such a service is vital if the company is to progress and remain competitive. The allocation of funds for this purpose may be the decision of the managing director after consultation with the board of directors. An industrial firm's library is sometimes managed by a small committee, but more usually it is the concern of one member of the board, such as the Director of Research, to whom the librarian will be directly responsible.

(ii) *Nationalised industries*
In these cases the libraries have been developed on a Civil Service pattern, being run without a library committee and with the librarian coming under the control of the Research Director. Ultimate responsibility will rest with the Minister of the Government; thus for example, the Minister of Power is answerable to Parliament for the library services of the Central Electricity Generating Board.

(iii) Research, trade and development associations

These are essentially autonomous bodies controlled and organised by the industries for whose benefit they exist. An information department performs a vital function in their activities and the libraries is a most important part of it. The librarian will therefore usually be a member of the staff of the Information Manager, or a similar senior executive responsible to the association's Council.

(d) LIBRARIES BELONGING TO PUBLIC AUTHORITIES

The libraries of the British Broadcasting Corporation and the British Overseas Airways Corporation, to give two examples, follow the general special library pattern. Each has many libraries which are part of the general information service, the overall responsibility for which rests with the boards specially appointed for their control.

PUBLIC LIBRARIES

In the United Kingdom the public libraries began in 1850 when the first legislation allowed towns to levy taxation for library purposes. Towns and villages, large and small, down to parishes were permitted to inaugurate a service under acts passed in the latter half of the last century. The 1919 Act not only allowed County Councils to provide a library service for those areas not served by existing authorities, but also for the transfer of library powers, by agreement, between county and urban authorities. This was the last piece of legislation concerning public libraries before the 1964 Act. It is important to remember that prior to this date all public library legislation was permissive, that is, was adopted by local authorities of their own volition. In England and

Wales, the competent authorities were the councils of administrative counties, county boroughs, non-county and Metropolitan boroughs, urban districts and a few parishes. Under the Local Government Act of 1933, any library authority could delegate all but its borrowing and rate-levying powers to a library committee, but such delegation did not allow it to repudiate its responsibility for the committee's actions, for at least two-thirds of the committee had to be members of the council, i.e. aldermen or councillors.

But it must be reiterated that before 1964 the provision of a public library service was optional and for example, it was not until 1943 that Swindon, which at that time had a population of 68,000, adopted the Acts. For nearly one hundred years after the passing of the first Public Libraries Act, Swindon people's library needs could only be met by the Mechanics Institution library established by the Great Western Railway. Nor did a local authority have a statutory duty to take its library service seriously. Tickhill Urban District Council, a small local authority in the West Riding of Yorkshire, adopted the Acts in 1907 and erected a public library building with money given by a benefactor named Henry Shaw in 1908. The library building cost £1,800, including the site. Yet Tickhill never bought any books, nor appointed any librarians, but only provided a few periodicals in one small room. Until the County Council took over the responsibility for the service in 1967, the main 'library' room was used for social activities, including school meals and bingo. Only local action could ever have remedied this situation, for no Government Department was officially concerned in any way with the provision of or the standard of the public library service.

The Public Libraries and Museums Act of 1964 introduces a new conception. The first sentence of Section 1 places the overall responsibility for the service on the shoulders of the Secretary of State of the Department of Education and

Science: 'From the commencement of this Act it shall be the duty of the Secretary of State to superintend and promote the improvement of the public library service provided by local authorities in England and Wales, and to secure the proper discharge by local authorities of the functions in relation to libraries conferred on them as library authorities by or under this Act.' Every library authority is required to provide such information and provide such facilities for inspection of library services, stock and records as may be required for this duty. To assist the Secretary in his task, the Act provides for the creation of two Library Advisory Councils, one for England and one for Wales and Monmouthshire, to advise on the provision and use of library facilities. In turn the Secretary of State must make an annual report to Parliament.

These simple clauses have transformed the whole picture of the government of public libraries. Instead of authorities giving as good or bad a service as they think they can afford, a central Government Department is charged with general superintendence, with powers of inspection, and is given two advisory boards (on which librarians are represented) to survey the whole development. In short, the service has become mandatory.

The 1964 Act is so important that students must examine it in detail and this is the appropriate place to outline its other provisions, all of which have a bearing on the government of public libraries.

Library authorities and areas. The Act defines library authorities as the councils of counties, county boroughs, London boroughs, the City of London and such non-county boroughs and urban districts as were library authorities when the Act was passed. Joint Boards may be set up by the agreement of two or more authorities. All parishes ceased to be library authorities from the 1st April, 1965, and their powers passed to the county councils in whose areas they were situated.

If a non-county borough or an urban district which is a library authority has a population less than 40,000 on the review date, the Secretary of State may, after consultation with the councils concerned, and if he thinks it would lead to an improvement in the library service, make an Order providing that the local authority concerned shall cease to be a library authority and transfer its functions to the County Council. The review date was 1st April, 1965, and at ten year intervals thereafter.

Conversely, if a non-county borough or urban district is not a library authority yet has a population over 40,000 on a review date, it may apply to become a library authority. Before determining such an application, the county council affected is consulted as to the effect on the county's service. Any non-county borough or urban district council may at any time resolve to relinquish its function as a library authority, and if the Secretary of State confirms this action by an Order the function passes to the County Council.

Standards of service. The Act refers to standards of service in a very broad way. They are, however, implicit in section 7 which states: 'It shall be the duty of every library authority to provide a comprehensive and efficient library service for all persons desiring to make use thereof, and for that purpose to employ such officers, to provide and maintain such buildings and equipment, and such books and other materials, and to do such other things, as may be requisite.' This Section makes it clear that pictures, gramophone records and films can properly be provided as well as books and other printed matter, which must be sufficient in number, range and quality to meet the general and special requirements of adults and children. It also emphasises the desirability of encouraging both adults and children to make full use of the library service and of giving advice as to its use.

Though library authorities have a duty to allow access to their libraries to all comers, their obligation to lend books extends only to those who live or work or study full time in their areas. Nevertheless, if they wish they have the power to allow persons outside these categories to become borrowers and every encouragement is given to adopt this wider view.

Charges for library services. No charge whatever can be made for the use of the library service by any local residents or by people working or studying in the area. Charges may, however, be made for special facilities such as loans of gramophone records or pictures, for notifying a reader of a reservation, or for failure to return borrowed articles by a given date, though the Secretary of State has power to limit them to a reasonable amount. Charges are also authorised for supplying (as distinct from lending) catalogues and other bibliographical material.

Library premises may be used for meetings and exhibitions, the showing of films and slides, musical performances, and other events of an educational or cultural character; charges for admission are authorised for these activities.

Library co-operation. For the first time co-operation between library authorities is made a statutory requirement; this to be achieved by the constitution of regional councils whose areas the Secretary of State has to determine. A scheme will be made for each designated region, which will have a library council constituted of representatives of each library authority and of other persons. It will be the Council's duty to make arrangements for facilitating the co-operation of authorities with one another and with other bodies having functions in relation to libraries. There is also statutory provision for a levy on authorities to meet the cost of these schemes, and for full co-operation of all libraries within regions and for co-operation between regions.

025 St62g
c.1

Library committees. In practice local authorities govern their public libraries through a library committee. The Local Government Act of 1933 permits a local council to appoint a committee for any general or special purpose and under the authority of this Act a separate library committee may be appointed. It is important to note that this legislation is permissive.

The Public Libraries and Museums Act of 1964 repealed that part of the 1919 Act under which County Councils were required to refer public library matters to their education committees and county borough councils were authorised to do so if they wished. Until the passing of the new law most, but not all, municipal authorities governed their libraries through a libraries committee, whereas all county authorities worked through county library sub-committees of the education committee. The new Act has left local authorities free to decide whether or not to set up a separate committee. This was not because there was any opposition to such appointments being made, but only on the grounds that the central government avoids telling local authorities how to run their affairs. Although the result of this is that there is now less uniformity and consistency of practice than before, it can be said that the majority of library authorities govern through a separate committee for library matters.

There has been no recent library legislation in Scotland and Northern Ireland and in these two countries the responsibility for the public library service still rests largely with local authorities. In Scotland it is a statutory requirement that a burgh council *must* annually appoint a library committee which has considerable powers as of right. On the other hand a county council derives its right to provide a library service from the Education (Scotland) Act 1962 and its education committee *may* appoint a library sub-committee to which it may delegate any of its functions.

The law in Northern Ireland is no more consistent, for

although the municipal authorities, the urban districts, boroughs and towns, *may* appoint a libraries committee, the counties *must* appoint one, the constitution of which is precisely prescribed. In 1964 responsibility for library matters was transferred from the Ministry of Health and Local Government to the Ministry of Education. Under existing legislation the library functions of the Ministry of Education are limited to approval of:

(a) the appointment and remuneration of county and county borough librarians and their deputies, whose qualifications and necessary experience it prescribes

(b) the relinquishing of powers and duties of urban district councils in favour of county councils

(c) loans for the provision of new buildings

(d) the acquisition, sale or exchange of land

(e) byelaws

It is interesting to note that the Northern Ireland Advisory Council was set up in 1949 as an independent body representative of professional librarians, university institutions and local authorities, with the object of considering measures for the development and expansion of library services. Though it had no powers, it exerted great influence and is an interesting precursor of the setting up of Library Advisory Councils for England and Wales in 1964.

In order to understand the position north of the border, the best introduction is still the Report of the Advisory Council on Education in Scotland on *Libraries, Museums and Art Galleries* issued in 1951; for Northern Ireland the Hawnt Report of 1966 is essential reading. Bibliographical details of both publications are given in the reading list.

2

Management

The first chapter of this book has attempted to define the governing bodies of libraries, to show where the ultimate responsibility for the development and government of libraries is to be found. But how does a governing body govern? What is involved in the management of libraries? Who controls the day to day work in libraries? This second chapter tackles these questions.

The Oxford English Dictionary gives many meanings for the word 'control'. In this context the two most relevant are 'to exercise power over' and 'to call for account'.

Control by the governing body. A governing body performs an act of control if it sets up a library committee and delegates to it all or any of the powers it may possess. The most obvious example is in local government where it is usual for a local authority to set up a library committee to be responsible for the control of its library service. There is, however, usually a limit to the committee's power and it is rare for a library committee to be able to authorise any capital expenditure without obtaining the approval of the full council of the local authority.

Similarly the selection and appointment of a librarian by a governing body of a library is another example of the 'exercise of power over' the library by its governing body. In all types of library the initial selection of a librarian may be delegated to a committee, but the final appointment is normally subject to the approval of the governing body. Again, in making policy decisions regarding a library, the governing body is 'exercising power' over the service. It should be clearly understood that the librarian's function is to recommend lines of action, i.e. policy, but it is the decision of the governing body that permits consequent action.

To give a simple example, a public librarian may feel that the time is opportune to set up a gramophone record service within the system he manages, but he must first recommend its provision as a desirable new development to the library committee who must also agree. Subsequently the full council of the local authority must approve the new policy and accept its financial implications.

A chief librarian is employed to manage or administer a library, to be responsible for carrying out the policy decisions of the governing body, which will seek his skilled advice but need not act upon it. Control is further exercised by the governing body by requiring him to present regular and special reports from time to time.

A library cannot operate without finance and this must be provided by the governing body. The amount allotted will be a policy decision based on a recommendation from the librarian. Even though the librarian is responsible for the spending of the library's funds, he is still subject to the control of the governing body because he is required to report regularly on his expenditure. This matter is dealt with at greater length in the next chapter.

Control by the librarian. While the governing body is responsible, usually legally, for the library's development, its policies and its finance, the librarian is selected and paid to carry out those policies. He plans and organises the service according to the policy already decided and the finance already provided, using to the best possible advantage the raw materials (books, periodicals, microfilms, manuscripts, etc.), a labour force (professional staff with supporting non-professional staff) and premises (library buildings) at his disposal.

The librarian's functions are to formulate policy; to plan the organisational framework; to make the major decisions; to supervise the senior staff such as heads of departments or branch librarians, seeing that they carry out properly the responsibilities allocated to them. He controls all the staff and their activities with the object of ensuring that his organisation functions with maximum efficiency. He has to be certain that the necessary stock is bought, that these purchases are adequately recorded and that they are subsequently made available for use at service points. The larger the library service the more complex will be the organisation, yet it always remains the librarian's duty to co-ordinate all the many parts, both human and material, that contribute to the end product, i.e. a good library service.

In all his activities the librarian is 'exercising power over' the library. For example:

(a) in his supervision of the selection of library materials, ensuring that the book stock is adequate to the needs of and appropriate to the constant changes in demand of the readers served.

(b) in planning the pattern of the organisation and its staffing. The duties and responsibilities of all staff have to be clearly defined. The librarian has to be responsible for all staff appointments and then for encouraging their initiative, developing their knowledge and ability and, of great importance, securing an adequate and fair salary for every person employed in his library.

(c) in reviewing the administrative routines of departments

so that every routine is carried out as simply as possible, examining every process to consider its necessity, eliminating all inessential work whether clerical or manual.

The 'control' of a library by a librarian is therefore a dynamic activity, and at this level three things are required; firstly, a constant inflow of information on which sound judgement can be based; secondly, the ability to see the needs of the library as a whole and unobscured by administrative detail; and thirdly, sufficient confidence and courage to give the necessary orders and leave others to carry them out. In addition, a librarian in exercising 'control' must have a sense of awareness that only comes from experience, for management is an art as well as a science. The action proposed in a particular situation must not only be supported by sound argument and appropriate information, but it must 'feel' right as well. It is invariably the qualities of sensitivity and foresight that make the good administrator.

The librarian's total activity may therefore be summed up as that of 'controller', exercising power over or managing the library, but always responsible to the governing body which must have the overhead or final responsibility for its control.

So far we have looked at the *principles* of control or management by governing bodies and by librarians and we must now consider the *methods* of library administration.

The Librarian. When policy has been decided it becomes necessary to ensure that an effective organisation exists to carry it out, subject always to sufficient central control being retained to ensure that any major departure from the original plan is referred back to the governing body for prior approval. The detailed execution of the plan is the function of management, which was defined by Urwick in his *Pattern of Management* as 'getting things done through people'. The chief librarian is the manager of a library. However much he may delegate, he is the director, the key man, the superintendent, the principal organiser and planner, the decider and always in the long run he is held responsible for all that goes on. The outstanding quality required of a director is leadership. He must, of course, have initiative, integrity and imagination, and above all, he must inspire confidence and personal respect. This can only be achieved if it is clear that he is prepared to accept responsibility at all times. A librarian who is known always to be willing to do this earns the full confidence of his staff.

There are many personal qualities that a librarian should possess, such as the ability to speak in public, to appreciate the capabilities of the members of his staff, to be resourceful in all situations, but two of very great importance are an ability to get on with people and a belief in his work. Without the former, any librarian will fail, for he has to deal daily with people; readers, staff, members of the governing body, a variety of persons for all of whom he must have a genuine feeling of friendliness and helpfulness. This last quality together with faith and conviction are essential attributes of a good librarian. It must be patently obvious to all he comes in touch with, that he cares passionately about his library and the service it gives.

The simplest form of library staff organisation is a pyramid of individual librarians, each with fairly well-defined responsibilities, from the junior professional librarian at the lowest level to the chief librarian at the top. At various levels in the chain of command there may also be found the specialist librarians whose job it is to provide expert advice, e.g. music librarians, children's librarians. These librarians may have subsidiary administrative responsibilities for their own section of the library's work, but they do not necessarily take a major part in the general managerial activities. Outside the main professional framework of library administration are the personal assistants, chief clerks and private secretaries of the most senior librarians. However, the success of a library depends primarily on the librarians in the administrative grade and, though delegation, co-operation, co-ordination, communication and good personal relationships (about all of which something is said elsewhere) are required at all levels, the basic requirement is clear direction from the chief librarian.

Delegation. Both chief librarians and their senior departmental librarians must delegate many responsibilities to other members of the staff. The chief delegates to the senior librarian who in turn pass on certain duties to assistant librarians. Failure here can lead to disastrous results. The selection of new book purchases for a library system should be a team effort; no chief librarian working on his own could carry it out properly. There was once a large municipal library in which the chief librarian (not even the chief cataloguer) personally checked all classification decisions and catalogue entries. The inevitable result was a serious bottleneck in the cataloguing department and, most serious of all, new books in urgent demand were held up for far too long.

If a senior librarian has authority delegated to him, then he must be prepared to make decisions within the limits of his responsibility and to report to the chief where necessary. It is equally important to note that the chief must accept his senior librarian's decisions and must be willing to risk occasional mistakes.

Another example of delegation is to be seen when the librarian gives one member, or a working party, of his staff, a special assignment, e.g. to produce a report on the microfilming of a run of an eighteenth century local newspaper, or to consider the effect in a county library on the transport schedules of delivery vans if and when an additional vehicle is purchased.

Planning. Librarians with senior executive responsibility are always thinking about what has been done or is to be done in the present situation and in the future. This is one of their particular duties, an activity which librarians should be doing all the time, not only when in the library but often in their off-duty time. It is a basic job and involves thinking about policy on a high level.

It is important to note that planning is concerned with the formulation of a programme that is based on an understanding or a conception of the real objectives of the library. This determination of the objectives or the functions of libraries, particularly public libraries, has been neglected in the past.

Co-operation. This follows naturally after delegation and planning. In a library organisation where there is real delegation of duties and responsibilities to senior staff, who are expected to play an active part in the planning of its future activities, there will certainly be co-operation between the chief and his executive staff. A live library is always changing in all sorts of ways. This change is barely perceptible to the reader who should only know of it as a smooth working and efficient organisation. But unless it becomes moribund and dead, it will be constantly evolving. In this situation, the reactions and co-operation of the staff are much better if they are kept informed about all aspects of the library so that they feel they have a share in forming new policy and reaching new decisions.

It follows naturally that free and frank opportunities for making suggestions and constructive criticism lead to staff enthusiasm, a factor which greatly helps the librarian in his task of leadership. Confidence in the chief grows when it is realised that he is interested in all matters and knows what is going on, that he understands the background to any suggestion and above all, that he takes action.

c

This is the thinking process which comes before action and can be divided into creative planning and routine planning and it is the former which is the more important, concerned as it is with deciding what is the objective to be attained and what are the resources available for its achievement.

Management aids or services. Libraries are now complex institutions and the complicated tasks facing librarians will continue to develop this way. This period of rapid technological change will call for new and improved services. At the same time social work is changing and increasing, children are to have a longer school life and for many more of them higher education in a college of further education or university. There is a trend towards larger local authorities, business corporations, and institutions of all kinds. These developments will demand from chief librarians and their immediate senior staff great skill in planning and organisation and in leadership. In addition, modern inventions, for example the more widespread use of computers, will bring some savings in time and labour for those library staff engaged in routine clerical work and in certain aspects of professional library work. These savings in time and labour are achieved by the proper use of what have come to be known as management services, which are listed below. Increasingly they will become part of the librarian's equipment, for in exercising his managerial responsibility he will be able to make decisions and to give an improved service to readers by being given detailed and accurate information more quickly. Thus the librarian in the future will find use for advanced management techniques of all kinds. These include organisation and methods investigations, work study and job evaluation, the elaborate techniques of cost-benefit analysis, operational research, regression analysis and critical path analysis. At a later stage the student will need to know more of these fascinating and exciting possibilities. It must be emphasised, however, that management services are merely new tools; they are not a substitute for good management but are invaluable aids to making decisions, securing value for money and the improvement of efficiency.

There are unfortunately many libraries which lag behind in this matter and others whose interest has not gone further than the review of elementary clerical procedures. This is a field in which there will be increasing co-operation and joint action, for all libraries must consider whether they can avoid duplicative effort and make better use of staff by centralising technical processes such as cataloguing and sharing other services, such as a specialist music librarian within a particular locality. It is almost impossible to lay down general rules in this matter, but though it is dealt with in more detail in the fourth chapter (on staffing) it is fundamental to reiterate that library operations should be carried out as efficiently as possible in order to avoid unnecessary wastage of staff time and that professional staff should not normally be asked to perform non-professional tasks.

3

Finance

This chapter deals with a supremely important subject, for finance is a fundamental moulding factor in the administration of libraries. Library services have to be paid for and since only in certain instances are they paid for by the recipient of the service, the cost of most libraries must be borne by the community, usually through a method of taxation. The size and quality of these services must rest upon the size and proportion of the resources that a community is prepared to expend upon them. If the administration of libraries is to be efficient, regard must be paid to the wise and proper spending of money, and it is therefore necessary to consider the various aspects of the source and control of their income and expenditure.

It is proposed to look first at the central government machinery and then examine later the financial control exercised by other bodies such as local authorities. In this respect the Treasury is the key department. Legally all the national revenue is the Queen's revenue, but the raising and spending of it is controlled by the House of Commons. It is important to remember that the greater part of government expenditure is authorised from year to year. The cost of defence, the social services and the country's administration are subject to the annual vote by the House of Commons to grant 'aids or supplies' to the Crown. The estimated total expenditure of these supply services, as they are called, is considered by Parliament in February each year. This means that each government department must submit its estimates of expenditure to the Treasury two or three months earlier. When the House of Commons has given its approval to these estimates, the amounts requested are distributed, subject to Treasury approval.

As was shown in the first chapter of this book, the central government of the country has a huge responsibility for libraries and it is for this reason that the student should understand the basic workings of its finance. The machinery for the central control of expenditure consists of the Treasury, the Comptroller and Auditor-General, the Select Committee on Public Accounts and the Select Committee on Estimates. Treasury control is continuous and all-pervasive; it is not only concerned with the departmental estimates as has already been mentioned, but its approval is required for all new expenditure. In addition, the Treasury prescribes the general rules to be observed by all government departments for financial and accounting procedure and its interest in a department's financial activities is continuous throughout the year. The rates of pay and numbers and grading of all staffs employed by the government departments are also the concern of the Treasury.

The Comptroller and Auditor-General is an official appointed by the Crown to serve Parliament and he has two functions. He authorises the release of money for government purposes and he audits the public accounts to ensure that it has been properly spent.

The Public Accounts Committee, a Select Committee established by Gladstone in 1861, exists to ensure that full value has been obtained for the money expended and to assess whether there has been waste and inefficiency. The other Select Committee, on Estimates, examines all estimates of expenditure and suggests economies.

Parliamentary control over all public expenditure is therefore very real.

Before dealing with the financial control of local authorities by the central government, it will be helpful at this stage to say something more about local government finance. Local authorities derive their income mainly from four sources:

(a) income from property
(b) charges for services
(c) grants from the central government
(d) rates

The first two produce only a small proportion of the total income, but grants-in-aid are vital, particularly in such services as education and health. The rate is the most important element in the sphere of local government finance. It is levied at so much in the pound on the net annual value of real properties, except where such have been specially de-rated, e.g. agricultural and industrial properties, or where they are not beneficially occupied. There are also certain special exemptions, such as schools and places of worship. Through the rating system, local authorities raise the money needed for their own purposes, except that in the county areas the rating authorities are the county districts, urban and rural. Thus the county councils obtain their funds through the county districts on whom they issue a precept for the amount needed. This precept must be added to the basic rate required by the collecting authority for its own purposes. This system avoids the drawback of confronting the citizen with more than one rate demand. It is important to note that local authorities have almost complete autonomy in the exercise of their rating powers which are not subject to any outside review.

Yet the system of central government finance has important repercussions on local authorities. Indeed the central control over local authority finance is comprehensive, e.g. (i) through grants, (ii) by audit, (iii) by way of loans.

(*i*) A very substantial part of their income is provided by Exchequer grants which are now paid by the Minister of Housing and Local Government in the form of *rate support grants* to local authorities in England and Wales under the Local Government Act of 1966. In order to arrive at the aggregate amount of rate support grants, the Minister has to determine the aggregate of Exchequer Grants to local authorities in respect of their *relevant* expenditure for the year. In considering this matter, libraries are reckoned to be one of the *relevant* services and expenditure on them is taken in account in deciding the amount of money granted. This practice was introduced for the first time with the Rate Support Grant Order for 1966 which gave a detailed account of the sums of money that it was proposed to grant to local authorities for the next two financial years, 1967–68 and 1968–69. In the future this annual report of the Minister of Housing and Local Government will be of great significance to the development of the public library service. It will be an indication of the rate of growth that is expected and the Order for 1966 reveals that the central government is making an allowance for an increase in the total expenditure on public libraries of 9 per cent for each of the two years in question. This is a new and an important factor which will have to be considered by committees and librarians.

The Local Government Act of 1958 allows the appropriate Minister to withhold or to reduce the grant payable to a local authority if he is satisfied that it has failed to achieve or maintain proper standards of service. It follows that the Department of Education and Science through the Secretary of State has the right to enquire into the efficiency of any public library, to inspect it and to make comments on it. A local authority may spend the money received from the rate support grant on any service it wishes and it can be said that this gives it greater freedom in the management of its finances; but the opportunity that these grants will give to the Department of Education and Science to review the reasonableness of the expenditure on and the efficiency of the public library service, added to the threat of the withdrawal of the grant if the service is not satisfactory, provides one of the most important methods by which the central government exercises influence over the operations of local authority library services.

(*ii*) The second method of financial control of local authorities by the central government is by the system of annual audit by district auditors appointed by the Ministry of Housing and Local Government. District, or external audit as its name implies, is an outside check on the local authority and its officers carried out by civil servants who are concerned with the accuracy of the accounts, the soundness of the supporting records, the correctness of payments, the proper custody of stores and precautions against fraud. It also acts as an assurance to the central government that the law relating to finance has been complied with and any expenditure incurred without statutory authority is disallowed by the auditor. Such illegal payments are surcharged personally upon those who authorised them, that is the members of the council concerned, not the officers.

(*iii*) No local authority has the financial resources to meet the cost of all its capital expenditure on buildings and equipment and from time to time the raising of money by way of loans is essential. In general, local authorities are only allowed to borrow money for work to be done which is of a permanent nature. The sanction of the appropriate Ministry must be obtained before borrowing and in the case of public libraries applications have to be submitted to the

Department of Education and Science. An application for
loan sanction for sites, buildings or equipment has to be
accompanied by a copy of the resolution of the Council
authorising it. In the case of buildings the following
information should also be provided:

(a) Explanation of the need for and description of the
project, i.e. new building, extensions, or adaptations; system
of construction etc.

(b) Confirmation that planning permission has been
obtained

(c) Gross cost of building and site works, stating whether
this is a final estimate or whether it is based on tender and,
in the latter case, whether the lowest tender has been
accepted and whether the tender price is fixed or variable

(d) Amount of professional fees payable (by individual
professions)

(e) Cost of furniture and equipment

(f) Amount of loan required; an explanation should be
given if this differs from the total anticipated cost of the
project

(g) Period desired for repayment for
   (i) Building
   (ii) Furniture and equipment

(h) Approximate date when building work will be started

It is therefore clear that central control over local authority
finance is comprehensive, especially as there is also a
statutory duty on all councils to keep accounts in an orderly
manner, and to make an annual return of income and expenditure to the Ministry of Housing and Local Government.

THE BUDGET

The budget is the focal point of the financial procedure of all
libraries. The annual estimate of the expenditure likely to

be incurred and of the income to be received is of tremendous importance. It should be seen primarily as a plan of action, as the decision on how a library is to continue to function and to develop during the coming year.

The terms 'budget' and 'estimates' can be regarded as synonymous but it is necessary to distinguish between

(a) *the revenue budget* which is what is usually meant by local authorities when referring to their 'estimates'. This is an annual estimate of the money necessary to meet the cost of the normal and regular requirements of the library service.

(b) *the annual capital budget.* Expenditure of a capital nature may be described as that which is incurred on a project of lasting value, even though that value may diminish in the course of time, whereas revenue expenditure is usually of a constantly recurring nature and produces no permanent asset. The cost of erecting a library is an example of capital expenditure producing an asset with a long life, whilst expenditure on the general maintenance of a library – staff salaries, books, heating, lighting and cleaning – is of a revenue nature. The annual capital budget shows the capital expenditure for one year ahead and is to be distinguished from

(c) *the long-term capital programme* which is a statement of projected capital works for a specific period usually three or five years ahead. In the case of libraries it is salutary for a librarian to have to make a reasonable forecast of the programme of new buildings required in the next five years. It does not authorise expenditure nor commit either the controlling body or the librarian, but it enables priorities to be decided and the financial implications of continuing development to be appreciated.

Consideration will now be given to the form of presentation

and method of construction of *the revenue estimates*. In practice, a great variety of forms are used but careful examination soon shows that the essential pattern is the same. The proposed expenditure for the ensuing year is set out in broad groupings, the most common being (i) staffing, (ii) books and other materials, (iii) maintenance of service including buildings, (iv) establishment expenses. The examples which follow show the development and sub-division of these items but it is useful to remember that all libraries consist of the Americans' three B's – books, brains and buildings – and they make up the total expenditure. For each item of expenditure there will be shown (a) the original estimate for the current year, (b) a revised estimate of probable actual expenditure for the current year, and (c) the estimate for the forthcoming year.

In addition, the actual figures of expenditure for the previous year or even years are often shown, and this is a practice which has much to commend it. Abnormal expenditure on an item in one particular year is more clearly shown; and the progress of expenditure (or lack of it) is better judged by an examination of the actual figures for two or even three years.

On page 44 is an example of the revenue budget of a public library authority.

A similar statement of estimated income must also be shown and the example given relates to that cited as a typical revenue budget:

1964–65 Actual income		1965–66 Estimate	1965–66 Probable	1966–67 Estimate
129	SALES	25	50	25
	FEES AND CHARGES			
2,014	Payments by other Authorities	2,210	2,210	2,310
7,554	Fines, etc.	8,300	8,100	9,000
309	RENTS	315	375	425
54	MISCELLANEOUS	60	60	60
£10,060		£10,910	£10,795	£11,820

	1964-65 Actual	1965-66 Estimate	1965-66 Probable	1966-67 Estimate
EMPLOYEES				
Pay				
Library Staff (librarians and clerks)	88,895	96,310	97,515	104,365
Other staff (manual workers)	13,922	14,475	14,935	17,175
National Insurance	4,676	6,545	6,595	6,825
Superannuation	5,814	6,090	6,135	6,680
PREMISES				
Upkeep of buildings and grounds	3,304	4,820	4,660	5,130
Fuel, light, cleaning materials and water	5,360	5,825	5,825	7,150
Rent and rates	5,822	6,050	5,990	7,560
SUPPLIES AND SERVICES				
Books and bookbinding	98,891	109,600	109,600	121,000
Gramophone records	1,103	1,975	1,975	1,710
Furniture, apparatus and equipment	1,416	5,850	5,695	1,815
TRANSPORT	3,777	3,850	3,995	4,410
CONTRIBUTIONS TO RENEWAL AND REPAIRS FUND	2,500	2,500	2,500	2,500
ESTABLISHMENT EXPENSES				
General office expenses	5,615	5,500	5,650	6,180
Travelling and subsistence	2,362	2,655	2,655	2,800
Proportion of cost of Central offices	13,249	14,795	21,660	20,090
Central and departmental establishment charges	3,793	3,920	4,275	4,290
AGENCY SERVICES	1,602	1,720	1,695	1,795
MISCELLANEOUS	539	730	700	795
DEBT CHARGES	12,871	16,325	16,150	19,385
REVENUE CONTRIBUTIONS TO CAPITAL OUTLAY				
Land and buildings	2,697	9,450	5,425	15,635
Private Architects, Fees	2,647	2,330	2,330	1,700
Proportion of cost of Architect's Department	3,195	4,225	1,810	1,050
Appropriation of assets	—		765	—
	£284,050	£325,540	£328,535	£360,040

At the time that it is presented to the library committee, an important part of the budgetary document is the short report of the librarian which is an explanation of the salient points of the statistical statement. It will set out and explain the differences between the estimates for the forthcoming year and those for the current year. Attention will be called to significant trends in expenditure and it can be invaluable in persuading the controlling body to provide money and the committee to support the claim.

We must now consider *capital estimates*, both the long-term capital programme and the annual capital budget. With regard to the former, the central government on more than one occasion has commended this practice to local authorities. In spite of the difficulties of preparing reliable figures, a reasonable forecast of the building programme of new branch libraries is very valuable to any public librarian. It enables him to determine the priority of different projects and to give warning of increasing annual loan charges and running costs.

On page 46 is an example of a long-term capital statement.

The annual capital estimates are a natural complement to the long-term capital programme. They are considered at the same time as the revenue budget because they affect it. Some capital items can be paid for from revenue as soon as they are provided, e.g. a mobile library, a small branch library building, replacement shelving for a central library, but the cost of many is met by borrowing the money which is repaid over a period of years. As mentioned earlier in this chapter, in the case of local authorities it is necessary to obtain the appropriate Government department's sanction for the raising of such a loan.

As these estimates relate to a single year, details are given of expenditure on (a) projects already begun, and (b) new schemes expected to be started in the forthcoming year. Before a scheme is included, its financial implications have usually been considered and approved in principle by the

Buildings

	Probable 1965-66	Estimate 1966-67	1967-68	Forecast 1968-69	1969-70
(i) BALANCES TO COMPLETE BUILDINGS					
Burton Joyce (£10,330)	870	—	—	—	—
Calverton (£9,830)	450	—	—	—	—
Carlton-in-Lindrick (£9,825)	1,280	—	—	—	—
Mansfield Woodhouse (£27,158)	44	—	—	—	—
Forest Town (£12,945)	545	—	—	—	—
Radcliffe-on-Trent (£12,275)	1,332	—	—	—	—
Ruddington (£10,652)	232	—	—	—	—
(ii) IN PROGRESS					
Keyworth (£13,175)	10,000	3,175	—	—	—
Kirkby (£44,615)	41,000	3,615	—	—	—
(iii) 1966-67 PROGRAMME					
Cotgrave (£11,000)	—	5,000	6,000	—	—
Kimberley (£17,500)	500	8,000	8,000	1,000	—
West Bridgford (£25,000)	—	10,000	14,000	1,000	—
(iv) FORECAST PROGRAMME					
1967-68 Bramcote (£16,000)	—	—	12,000	4,000	—
Bingham (£25,000)	—	—	15,000	10,000	—
East Leake (£14,000)	—	—	5,000	9,000	—
1968-69 Beeston (£30,000)	—	—	—	20,000	10,000
Blidworth (£15,000)	—	—	—	10,000	5,000
Edwinstowe (£11,000)	—	—	—	5,000	6,000
1969-70 Langold (£8,000)	—	—	—	—	4,000
Ravenshead (£16,000)	—	—	—	—	10,000
Eastwood (£20,000)	—	—	—	—	15,000

controlling body. Where this is not so, special attention must be drawn to it, because the mere inclusion of an item in the capital estimates does not constitute any authorisation of expenditure. Capital estimates are far less accurate than revenue estimates because the pace of the completion of work is difficult to predict. Nevertheless even though the effect of inaccuracies is not very great, the compilation of this side of the estimates must be carried out as realistically as possible.

On page 48 is an example of a capital budget statement.

Although the practice in every library will be varied to suit local circumstances, there are some basic principles in the preparation of budgets that should be stated. It is a process that starts at least three or four months before the commencement of the financial year and is a task which the librarian and the financial officer undertake together. The latter brings to bear his expert knowledge, skill and information of the controlling body's finances, while the former declares the needs of the library service expressed in terms of money. The compilation of the budget must be carried out with great care and responsibility. No figures should be included that cannot be supported by detail or that are arithmetically unreliable; all calculations should be agreed with the finance officer.

In the case of public libraries the draft statement of the proposed estimates of income and expenditure is first presented to the library committee meeting. This is the librarian's greatest opportunity to say what he thinks are the real requirements of his department. If his draft budget has been carefully drawn up and based on the policy decisions already made by the committee it will not be altered other than by minor changes, and having been approved it will go forward as a recommendation to the finance committee. It is very desirable that the financial officer shall be present at this meeting in an advisory capacity. Not only is it invaluable for the library committee to be warned that its proposals

Sites	Total cost	Paid	1965–66	1966–67	1967–68
SCHEMES ALMOST COMPLETED PRIOR TO 1.4.65	6,235	—	2,235	4,000	—
Erections	92,998	88,876	4,122	—	—
Furniture and Equipment	1,942	1,752	190	—	—
1964–65 PROGRAMME	—				
Keyworth					
Erection	13,175	—	10,000	3,175	—
Furniture and Equipment	2,350	—	200	2,150	—
Kirkby-in-Ashfield					
Erection	44,615	—	41,000	3,615	—
Furniture and Equipment	7,500	—	500	7,000	—
1966–67 PROGRAMME					
Cotgrave					
Erection	10,000	—	—	4,000	6,000
Furniture and Equipment	2,500	—	—	—	2,500
West Bridgford Extensions					
Erection	25,000	—	—	2,000	23,000
Furniture and Equipment	6,000	—	—	—	6,000
MINOR WORKS					
Garage at Ollerton	1,785	—	1,700	85	—
Garage at Balderton	1,200	—	600	600	—
Balderton – Heating Improvements	900	—	—	900	—
PURCHASE OF NEW VEHICLE	900	—	—	900	—
	£217,100	£90,628	£60,547	£28,425	£37,500

may not be financially attainable, but it is very necessary to know that a new policy is not seen to create financial difficulties.

In non-public libraries, the librarian's concern with finance is usually limited to the expenditure on staffing and books, other items such as were included in the example of a public library revenue budget being the responsibility of the finance officer of the organisation. In this respect the position of universities is important. Each university receives from the Treasury an annual grant based on an estimate made every five years and allocated by the University Grants Committee. The proportion of the total sum available to a university spent on libraries varies according to the size of the university and to other factors. At one time it was suggested that this amount should not be lower than four per cent, but as library costs, especially on books, periodicals and bookbinding, may rise faster than other university costs, the allocation of a fixed percentage of university revenue may fall behind events and lead to a deterioration of standards of provision.

This annual sum of money for books, journals, binding and sundries is generally known as the recurrent grant, i.e. the basic funds used for the upkeep of stock. Not only universities, but every institution that maintains a library must from time to time make non-recurrent grants for new and special interests. In universities, for example, there is a paramount need to provide funds for basic collections of undergraduate and research material for newly established departments or faculties, for new courses or new lines of research material in existing departments and for special and rare items in the second-hand market or from the libraries of collectors or distinguished scholars.

In special libraries an annual budget is very desirable because long-term planning and efficiency are impaired unless there is certainty of regular and adequate finance,

D

but unlike public libraries, special librarians and information officers are usually only concerned with expenditure on stock and staff as the cost of heating, rent and other general expenses are the responsibility of other officers in the organisation. In this type of library a more than usually high proportion of the material acquired will be in the form of pamphlets, reports and periodicals. The amount of cataloguing, classification and indexing that needs to be carried out is much higher than in a general library and therefore the proportion of the budget spent on staff salaries is consequently considerably greater – a percentage of more than sixty-five rather than fifty which is common in public libraries.

4

Staffing

The main objective of a librarian is to provide his readers with a service of the highest possible standard. To do this he needs staff in the right numbers, with the necessary education, qualifications and training. Although staff selection, training and management are equally necessary in all types of library, large or small, the degrees of organisation and planning will vary with the size of the library. But personnel management is of great importance to the chief librarian whether his library is a small special library (e.g. in an architect's office) or a public library such as Lancashire County Library which employs nearly five hundred librarians and assistants or a gigantic organisation like the Library of Congress in the U.S.A. with a staff of over three thousand.

THE PRINCIPLES OF PERSONNEL MANAGEMENT

Staff management is concerned with finding the best available people to do the jobs which are necessary and then with helping them to make their maximum contribution to the service provided by the library. The well integrated efforts of the librarians and other staff reflect good management and

51

result in the maximum of productive work at every level. The ability and devotion of the staff largely determine the success of a library. It is hardly necessary to emphasise this point when it is realised that one of the main items of expenditure in any library budget is on staffing costs. In public libraries the cost of salaries and wages of the employees is usually at least 50 per cent of the total expenditure.

The basic requirements of good staff management would appear to be:

(a) the establishment of a clear chain of command
(b) making known the required task
(c) the delegation of responsibility for carrying it out.

As the objective of every library should be to give its readers the best possible service, any plan for management must start by reviewing the library as a whole, in particular by looking at the readers and deciding how their needs can be met. Then an analysis must be made of the staff duties called for and of the routines and other tasks that have to be performed. In the case of many libraries, especially those which are open longer than normal office hours (i.e. 9 a.m. to 5 p.m.) it is necessary to know how frequently these tasks are performed and over what span of time. In business management this operation is termed *job analysis*, which is by no means only concerned with determining salary scales, but is basic to the organisation of a library. In every library a statement has to be prepared of the number and kinds of posts that have to be filled with definitions of each of their duties and responsibilities. This schedule of posts which is generally known as the *establishment* is by no means static for as a library develops, it has to be changed to meet new and changing demands. For example, the introduction of mechanical equipment may lead either to a reduction in the number of clerical workers or to a redeployment of profes- sional librarians, or possibly to both. Similarly, extensions to a library service inevitably lead to a need to employ more staff.

It is important that each member of a library staff should be enabled to understand how his own job, however small, fits into the work of the library as a whole. An employee can give of his best only if he can see some point and purpose in what he has been asked to do. It must be clear to him that his task is one that matters and that the chief librarian is confident of his being able to perform it satisfactorily. There is nothing more conducive to bad work than a belief that a particular task has no real purpose and is not really necessary. This is expecially true of the routine tasks undertaken by non-professional library staff, and senior librarians should dispel such notions with clear explanations and proper briefing.

If a chief librarian is to be sure of the ability and work of his staff, he must take them into his confidence by attempting to give each individual member a wider picture of the library's work. This will help to make them feel a real part of the library and will lead to genuine pride in and devotion to the work; which is the main aim of staff management.

Each member of a staff should be doing a job to the upper limit of his capabilities. This is best achieved by giving each a responsibility that can just be fulfilled and then leaving the employee freedom within certain limits to get on with his own work. At the same time each employee should know the person above him to whom he can refer problems which are beyond his own powers to solve. Hence the need for an establishment or responsibility chart, about which more will be said later in this chapter.

In brief, the purpose of sound staff management can be defined as ensuring that everyone in the library, the staff at every level, knows beyond question who serves whom, who instructs whom, and who does what. Doubt and equivocation breed inefficiency.

STAFF ESTABLISHMENTS

The establishment of a library is its authorised complement of staff. The governing body of a library can alter its staff establishment at any time but it is usual for it to be reviewed on a regular basis, in many public libraries at least annually for minor amendments and additions and comprehensively every two or three years, when the library committee is called upon to consider the staffing position and to make recommendations both with regard to numbers of staff and levels of remuneration. Quite simply it is a list of all the posts, and the salary the holder of each post is to be paid, that the governing body has agreed shall be filled to ensure the proper running of the library. It can usually be expressed in terms of a chart which shows the posts and their relationship to one another. For identification purposes each post is often given a symbol and a job description. Examples both of establishment charts and job descriptions are given later, but it is necessary first to consider the posts which are to be found on library establishments. This is a matter on which it is difficult to generalise for the staffing arrangements in libraries are marked by great diversity, for no two libraries are alike, not even within the same type. Differences of practice are to be found in almost any two libraries, whether they be national, public, university or special, but very generally library staff establishments comprise three broad classes of posts – (a) professional; (b) pre-professional; (c) non-professional.

PROFESSIONAL POSTS FALL NATURALLY INTO THREE GROUPS:

(i) those above the level of head of a department within a library

(ii) those at the level of departmental head

(iii) those below departmental head level

Within these three groups there are five broad categories of professional library posts which can be classed as follows:

(i) *Above departmental head*
   (1) Librarian
   (2) Deputy Librarian
   (3) Principal Assistant Librarian

(ii) *At departmental head*
   (4) Senior Assistant Librarians

(iii) *Below departmental head*
   (5) Assistant Librarians

It is now necessary to deal more fully with these five categories of professional librarian.

(1) *Librarian*

This is the principal officer in a library service. In academic libraries he is usually styled simply as *the* Librarian, but in other types of library where it is felt appropriate to indicate that there are many librarians employed or several service points under his control Chief Librarian is a common designation. This title is also used by public library authorities, but it is more usual to indicate the type of authority served in the officer's title, e.g. City Librarian, Borough Librarian, County Librarian. In a few authorities the chief officer has additional responsibilities such as museums, art galleries or archives and he is styled the Director, e.g. in Cheshire, Herefordshire and Sunderland.

The chief librarian's first duty is to act as the professional adviser to the controlling body, normally through its library committee, on matters of policy and service development. After consideration of the librarian's recommendations, the managing body will formulate its policy and it is then the librarian's duty to carry it out. The librarian must identify himself closely with the community he serves. In all types of library, he must be aware of the many facets of local life, the habits, movements, interests, facilities, commerce, industry and so on, in order to be able to offer sound advice on the needs of the library. This advice may cover such different matters as the necessity for further library buildings, extensions or alterations to existing premises, the need for additional staff, revision of the rules and regulations governing the use of the library, the desirability of establishing special projects and new developments, for example, the arrangement of a series of special lectures and exhibitions, the microfilming of local newspapers or the installation of coffee vending machines in all branch libraries. Through his community awareness the librarian will be able to advocate these projects to his committee at appropriate times and he will present reports which outline the reasons for his proposals and in particular include a detailed costing of any scheme. In short the chief librarian's first function is to advise the governing body so that it can decide on the overall objectives and policies of the library.

Secondly, the chief librarian determines the organisational framework. He decides how the whole work of the library shall be divided into departments or sections. He makes clear the duties and responsibilities of each department. This is a continuing task because new developments will necessitate modifications and alterations.

Thirdly, in all matters the chief librarian makes the major decisions, including those concerned with staffing matters. He must be in the closest touch with his 'middle-management' heads, the senior librarians (these are indicated later in this chapter) and he must supervise their work to ensure that they are carrying out the responsibilities that have been delegated to them. However large the library system the librarian can never avoid having to take the responsibility for all that happens, good and bad, fortunate and disastrous. In the long run it is almost inevitably his initiative that assures the success of the library. Failures are his fault and he must neither blame his masters, i.e. the council or management committee, nor his servants, i.e. his staff, every one of them from the top to the bottom of the organisation.

(2) *The Deputy Librarian* is the Chief Librarian's *alter ego*, a senior partner rather than a subordinate. If both the chief and his deputy carry out the partnership properly, the members of the governing body, both individually and in library committee, the staff and all other persons with whom the library has to co-operate, should be equally happy to accept the advice and decision of either. The relationship is intimate, and for that reason must be on the right basis. Each partner has something of the disadvantages; the deputy may have the detailed cares, but the chief is left to make the decision on the stickiest problems; the deputy has to act as a buffer between the world and the chief, but the latter has to take the final responsibility; the deputy does much of the work and receives too little credit for it, but the chief has to bear any opprobrium for the deficiencies of the service. It is important that the deputy is kept acquainted with all matters of importance, is consulted on major matters, is supported whenever he has to take decisions in the chief's absence and is given a proper share of privileges. On the other hand, the deputy must be loyal at all times and keep the chief fully acquainted with his decisions.

As the chief librarian's understudy, the deputy takes complete charge in his absence. He attends major committee meetings with him and other committees in his stead. He will, of course, have responsibility for certain aspects of the library's work; this has to be decided by the chief, but it is important that in these matters the deputy takes decisions, only consulting the chief over difficult problems and projected changes of policy. Though the deputy will filter many matters put forward for consideration by the chief, he must not become a bottleneck. To make a rule that every-

thing must pass through the deputy is unsound, for the
chief librarian should quite properly deal from time to time
with other senior staff. Both chief and deputy should ensure
that decisions are taken as quickly as possible for few
administrative problems are so grave that they have to be
thought over for a lengthy period.

It is an interesting feature of the deputy system that it
works better if the chief has no high level personal assistant
or staff officer or even a secretary. If he does, the closeness
of the relations between him and his deputy cannot be
properly maintained. He will find it difficult not to make
comments and to share confidential opinions with one of
these officers rather than with the deputy, thus undermining
the deputy's position. It is therefore best that the chief and
deputy share the services of administrative clerks and
assistants, but if the chief finds it necessary to have a personal
assistant then it should be a relatively junior officer who is
kept in the background.

(3) *Principal Assistant Librarian* In some libraries the designation of this post indicates that the holder is next in rank to
the Librarian but that he is not empowered to 'deputise' or
to act for the Librarian in his absence, but it is more commonly used to indicate the 'third man' in the hierarchy and
in this case Chief Assistant Librarian and Assistant County
Librarian are sometimes found as variants. It also indicates
a level of officer who is below the rank of Deputy but above
that of Departmental Head: for example, Superintendent of
Branch Libraries; Chief Administrative Assistant; Staff
Training Officer; Chief Bibliographical Assistant; District or
Regional Librarian; Organiser of Work with young people
and/or schools.

(4) *Senior Assistant Librarians* can be defined as those members
of a library staff holding important positions, who rank below

the deputy but have duties and responsibilities that clearly place them above the junior professional or assistant librarian level.

In university libraries members of staff in this class are usually termed sub-librarians and in public libraries they are the librarians who are in charge of separate departments or sections of the system, e.g. Reference; Central Lending; Cataloguing; Stock editor; Book acquisitions; Regional, District, Area or Branch Library; Technical Library; Commercial Library; Music Library; Local and any other special collections; Hospital library; Prison library; Mobile library service; Visual aids; Binding; Extension activities.

(5) *Assistant Librarians* This group comprises all the librarians who rank below the level of head of a department or special service within a library. They will be found in most of the departments listed in the previous paragraph serving as 'deputies' or with specific responsibilities. Examples include: Reader's adviser; Gramophone Record librarian (within a Music Department); Mobile librarian; Children's librarian; Branch librarian; Inter-library loans; Periodicals librarian; Cataloguer.

Having written at some length about the professional staff it is necessary to mention the other two broad classes of posts, the pre-professional and the non-professional.

The PRE-PROFESSIONAL class comprises posts which are occupied by graduates and non-graduates who possess at least the minimum pre-entry qualification prescribed by the Library Association for sitting the professional examinations. Persons in this class should be designated as trainee librarians. They will normally work for twelve months before being sent to a course of full-time study at a school of librarianship.

The term NON-PROFESSIONAL is used to denote all other

members of a library's staff establishment (and numerically these are likely to be the majority) who are not professional librarians. They are employed to carry out either routine or specialist duties and this class includes clerks, assistants, binders, machine operators, typists, accountants, artists, administrative assistants, porters, packers, drivers. In the constant search for general efficiency they play a vital part and the chief librarian must be concerned not only with fixing the total number of staff employed but also with the allocation of work between the professionals and the non-professionals. He must closely examine the work of the library in order to identify the tasks best carried out by clerks, technicians and lay administrative officers. It is important that professional librarians should be relieved of non-professional duties not only in their own interests but for the benefit of the service. The widest possible use of non-professional staff permits the fullest use of professional manpower and gives better opportunities and greater satisfaction to both groups of staff.

A staff establishment can be shown in the form of a chart and because of limited space the examples selected have been restricted to (a) a small university library and (b) a County Library Headquarters.

The establishment records in a library will include a description of the duties attaching to every post that has to be filled. The following are examples of such 'job' descriptions:

Regional Children's Librarian
In charge of junior library at Regional Library and supervises children's sections in other branch libraries within the region. Responsible for primary school library service. Selects all children's stock and allocates to branch libraries and school stock. Advisory duty to children in

(a) UNIVERSITY LIBRARY

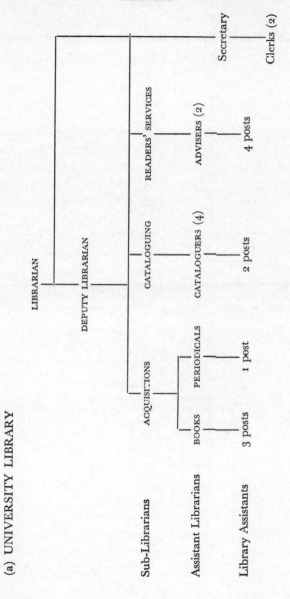

LIBRARIAN

DEPUTY LIBRARIAN

Secretary

Clerks (2)

Sub-Librarians — ACQUISITIONS, CATALOGUING, READERS' SERVICES

Assistant Librarians — BOOKS, PERIODICALS, CATALOGUERS (4), ADVISERS (2)

Library Assistants — 3 posts, 1 post, 2 posts, 4 posts

(b) COUNTY LIBRARY HEADQUARTERS

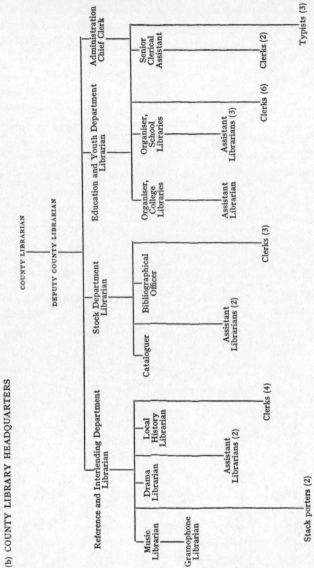

libraries and to teachers regarding organisation of school libraries. Arranges book displays and promotes extension activities, e.g. story hours, talks, National Library Week.

Music Librarian
Responsible for selection of all scores and books on music. Makes all classification and cataloguing decisions for new additions to stock in this field. Advises generally to individuals, groups and other senior librarians. Promotes service with lists, exhibitions, gramophone recitals, etc. Supervises Gramophone Record Librarian.

Chief Cataloguer
Responsible for the classification of books and the maintenance of all catalogues in the library.

Mobile Librarian
In charge of the mobile library service, including the work of the driver. Travels on vehicle acting as reader's adviser seven days in each fortnight. Responsible for book stock and readers' requests. Carries out regular reviews of all routes and timetables.

IN-SERVICE TRAINING

The 1962 report of a Library Association committee on In-Service Training defines this as 'implying the imparting by direct methods (which may include lecturing to groups) of informed experience within a specific library system'. In other words, it is concerned with the training of staff to ensure their greater efficiency in the library in which they are employed and it is not carried out for the benefit of the individuals concerned. Because its object is to improve the quality of the work performed by members of a library's staff, its justification is an economic one and it is therefore applicable to every type and size of library. The smaller the library the more informal is the staff training, but conversely the larger the library the greater the need for an organised system.

In all libraries large enough to call for a planned in-service training scheme, the staff under consideration may be divided into the following groups:

(i) trainee librarians, those who are working and gaining some practical experience before entering a full-time librarianship course at college.

(ii) professional librarians, particularly newly qualified persons working for the first time in posts of some responsibility, but also newly appointed senior staff.

(iii) non-professional assistants, both full-time and part-time.

(i) The training of trainees or pre-professional librarians has two vitally important implications for the persons involved. It enables them to make certain that they have chosen the right career for themselves and it develops their personalities by bringing them into contact with the reality of life within a library. The new relationships that have to be met, both in serving readers and in working alongside other people, have a most maturing effect. From the point of view of the employing library it is highly desirable that the number of trainees shall be sufficient to enable them to be regarded as a group, from six to eight people has been found to be very suitable, and that they be appointed as supernumary to the normal establishment. This makes it possible for the group to meet for lectures and discussions, and for individuals to be assigned to a wide variety of duties not only in their own libraries but also in other neighbouring libraries, bookshops and colleges.

The scheme for trainees should be as intensive as possible and planned for the needs of each member of the group. Though its primary aim is to attempt to ensure that the trainees are familiar with every aspect of the library service (which means that they work for a short while in every department and section) an effort should be made to increase the general knowledge and broaden the background of each participant. As far as possible trainees should attend every library event that takes place – the official opening of a new branch library, a children's book week, a gramophone recital, professional meetings, committee meetings.

Though it is not always easy to draw the line between training and education, care should be taken not to encroach into the latter field. It does not help if when the student gets to college, he feels that he is faced with repetitive lectures and studies.

(ii) Very few library school leavers have had much practical experience. Even those who worked in a library for up to a year before entering college often feel out of touch on their return and they will often find the challenge of a new post just as difficult to meet as the younger person finds the transition from school to work. Newly qualified staff, the junior professionals, need a great deal of help as they learn to undertake a practical job and as they try to understand the nature of the library system which they have joined. As they will generally have been appointed to specific posts, they should be initiated into their responsibilities by means of attachment to a more senior librarian who will act as supervisor as the necessary professional tasks are tackled. At every stage they should be encouraged to make suggestions and to attempt to apply the theoretical knowledge gained at library school to the new job in hand. As they will also sometimes be more familiar with modern techniques than

E

their seniors, this should be advantageous to the system as well as helping the young professional to identify himself in a real way with his new library.

Newly appointed senior staff are often left to find their own way around on the wrong assumption that as they have had previous experience in other libraries, they need no instructions in tackling a new job. Certainly they will be able to find out the essential details for themselves, but no two library systems are alike and positive steps must be taken to make sure that new senior librarians are quickly acquainted with the policy and practices of their new library. It is important that the chief librarian should if possible take a large part in this work, especially such aspects as the personal introduction of a new man to senior colleagues and other people it is important to know.

(iii) Many non-professional assistants will be appointed as school leavers and the first few weeks 'at work' is often a period of adjustment which imposes considerable strains, both physical and mental. It will help greatly if each new member of staff receives a leaflet giving conditions of employment (method of payment of salary, annual leave, sickness regulations, etc.) and an outline of the library, its purpose and services. As soon as possible after taking up their appointments, new entrants should undergo a general induction course which will tell them more of the organisation and their place in it. Right from the day they start, non-professional assistants have to be trained in the routines of their jobs. As these routines will frequently be specialised, it is important that the instruction shall be given by a senior non-professional rather than by a librarian, and never by another assistant. Routine practices should never be passed on by one assistant to another.

The training of part-time non-professional staff must not

be neglected. The employees in this group are usually older, more mature and less likely to resign after working for a few years. They are generally very interested in their work and respond more readily and with greater understanding to an organised training programme.

PROFESSIONAL AND NON-PROFESSIONAL DUTIES

In 1962 the Library Association approved and published its *Professional and non-professional duties in libraries; a descriptive list*. In the same year the Ministry of Education Working Party report on *Standards of public library service* dealt with this matter and in the first instance it agreed that the Roberts Committee's minimum standard requiring 40 per cent of the non-manual staff to be qualified librarians was appropriate for municipal libraries serving up to about 100,000 population and for county public libraries where the majority of the staff are normally employed in small units. It then went on to assert that in urban areas of concentrated populations, where there are large central libraries and several large or medium sized branches, there is greater scope for the economical use of qualified staff and that a ratio of about 33 per cent could be regarded as a reasonable minimum. It further suggested that this ratio might be reduced in the very largest cities, but that a figure of less than 25 per cent would be thought of as unsatisfactory in any library system.

It is now generally accepted that professional people should follow their profession at least to the extent that the major part of their time should be spent on professional work. This view is confirmed by a statement in Circular no. N.O.194 issued by the National Joint Council for Local Authorities in July 1966 that 'local authorities are to make the fullest possible use of library assistants, clerical and other staff on work which need not be performed by qualified librarians'.

What are professional duties? The Library Association descriptive list referred to earlier defines them as 'those whose adequate performance involves the ability to exercise independent judgment based on an understanding of the principles of library service – publication and information, users and the means by which they are brought into effective relationship. This understanding implies a wide knowledge of specific library techniques and procedures. This is not to say that specific techniques classified as professional cannot be taught to individuals who are not, by training, professional librarians. What is implied is that the adequate performance of the full range of professional duties requires professional judgment and a thorough understanding of the principles and objectives of each duty and its function in relation to the over-all purpose of libraries.'

In most special libraries where the size of the staff makes it possible, duties are clearly separated into professional and non-professional. This is especially true of government libraries where it has only been possible to grade posts in professional librarian grades in cases where there could be no doubt as to the nature and responsibility of the work. In most other non-public libraries the economic factor soon forced the employment of clerical workers at clerical rates of pay for clerical work.

RECRUITMENT

A most important result of good personnel administration is the satisfactory recruitment of new members of staff of high quality. Each vacancy that occurs presents an opportunity to strengthen the staff by a wise appointment. It is inevitable that some mistakes will be made in staff selection and, as each error lowers the morale of the rest of the staff and the effectiveness of the service, the chief librarian should be wise enough to use all possible devices to avoid making a bad choice. The quality of the person appointed to any vacancy can be no higher than the quality of those who can be persuaded to apply. The efforts to secure outstandingly good recruits at all levels demand that careful thought, ingenuity and planning are brought to bear in filling every post. The present trends in the advertisements of vacant situations in newspapers and periodicals demonstrate this fact. With the present manpower shortage, employing authorities are forced to make considerable efforts to make a vacant post as attractive as possible.

Regarding *professional* appointments, chartered librarians are more likely to apply for a position in a library of above average reputation where they are assured of being given fully professional duties, stimulating and challenging assignments, a chance to use initiative and to exercise responsibility. A library in this category will often be well known from its publicity and performance, and it will be discernible from the tone of its advertisements and its staff selection procedures that it offers opportunities for worthwhile work. In order to recruit suitably experienced chartered librarians, all types of libraries find it essential to 'sell' themselves. The current advertisement pages of library appointments in the *Times Literary Supplement* are very different from those of ten years ago.

TRAINEE LIBRARIANS are recruited from the ranks of university graduates and of school and college leavers with Advanced Level passes. Librarians must do more than advertise in local newspapers and use the Youth Employment Service to bring vacancies to their notice. They should prepare suitable publicity material emphasising that employment in a library has much to offer in terms of salary, training and prospects, printed in an attractive form and made available to headmasters and at careers conventions. Similarly it is essential that undergraduates should be made to realise that libraries have worthwhile careers to offer and that the University Appointments Officer should understand this and be in possession of the correct information. Here again the quality of the publicity material is important. Graduates should be given a comprehensive picture of librarianship and of individual libraries, with detailed information about the type of work, prospects and training.

NON-PROFESSIONAL STAFF are appointed with or without passes in the General Certificate of Education. In the past there has often been a high turnover rate in their numbers largely because librarians have tended to recruit from school leavers. This situation should alter as the training and prospects for non-professional workers are improved; the proposed Library Assistant's Certificate which will be obtained by passing examinations of the City and Guilds of London Institute should be a considerable help in this direction.

Like most employers, librarians have become less reluctant to consider 'over 45' workers for clerical and non-professional posts. Experience has demonstrated that they need not fear that such people will be set in their ways, slow to learn routines or unprepared to take instructions from younger persons. On the other hand it has been found that older persons can possess many desirable qualities – maturity of outlook and a greater sense of responsibility, a genuine interest in the job – and there is far less turnover than is the case with younger persons. Their use as part-time staff has also been realised in all types of libraries for providing extra clerical and counter assistance at the busiest periods, for evening and week-end duties and for occasional jobs of a repetitive and routine nature, e.g. in connection with stock taking.

5

Stock Control

Any attempt to define stock control reads almost like a statement of the meaning and basic purpose of librarianship, for it is usually taken to be concerned with the professional, clerical and manual tasks involved in attempting to solve the problems concerned with the selection, acquisition, preservation and deployment of the books and related media in libraries. Selection is the most important of these tasks, and though there will be variations of practice according to the type of library, whether academic, special or public, the determining factor common to all libraries is the amount of money available.

In some ways the book vote is the most curious of all items of a library budget, since many of the books for the purchase of which the money has been allocated, do not yet exist. They are no more than many thousands of forthcoming titles that may or may not have been announced by publishers, and though a librarian spends some money on books in print and on second-hand purchases for basic stock of new libraries or for replacement copies in larger libraries, he plans to buy mainly new books. How then, in considering estimates of expenditure, can a librarian really know in advance how much money will be needed to buy new books which will be published in the next financial year?

The short answer is, of course, that he does not know. With the exception of standing orders for annuals, or multi-volume works with firm publication schedules, and replacements or duplicates of books at present in stock, he can only have the vaguest notion of how he will spend the book fund in the coming months. Suppose, for example, a library has a special concern in the field of linguistics, this means that the librarian will wish to have as comprehensive a coverage of new titles on this subject as is possible. Yet a comparison of the number of books published on this subject from year to year shows a wide variation. According to figures published in the *Library Association Record* for August 1966, during the financial year 1964–65 there were 575 books which could be included in the Dewey main class 400, but in the next year 1965–66 the number of titles fell to 298, a substantial decrease. Not only do the number of new titles in each subject field vary from year to year, but the average price per volume also changes. Quoting from the same issue of the *Library Association Record*, in 1964–65 books on languages cost an average of 11s. 4½d. while in 1965–66 the price more than doubled to £1 2s. 11½d. In no other area of public or institutional expenditure do such irregular, indeed almost bizarre conditions exist. Even though the case quoted is extreme and the rather vague meaning of the Dewey Class 400 taken into account, this is evidence enough of the variabilities of the book world.

The whole matter is even more complicated by the uncertainties and irregularities of the publishing world, especially the unreliability of publication dates and speed of supply after an order has been placed. There is no guarantee that a book which has been ordered in a particular financial year will in fact be supplied during that year. Books can and frequently do become unavailable for a period of time; even shortly after publication date, a publisher will report 'temporarily out of stock' or 'reprinting, no date'. To order a book well in advance of publication might on the face of it seem a simple way round this difficulty, but it is the common experience of librarians that orders can and do remain in the order file from one year to the next. The reason is simply that publication dates are anything but firm; a book announced as forthcoming in six months time may possibly not appear for another year or more, and on occasion be withdrawn from publication altogether.

Despite all these anomalies most librarians are able to work within the limitations of the annual budgeting procedures which are imposed by the holders of the purse strings and are necessary to good management. The estimates for the required expenditure for the book fund are drawn up well in advance of the start of the financial year and it is wise to start thinking about next year's book requirements almost as soon as the amount for the present year has been approved. It is even better not to look at each year's book spending in isolation, but to place the estimated expenditure for each year in the context of a planned development over a fairly long period of time. (The five-year plan is one of the most useful procedures to be learned from the practice of the Soviet Union.)

In order to determine the cost of buying additions to stock, a librarian needs to know two factors, the number of volumes to be purchased and the average price of books. In spite of difficulties mentioned earlier it is possible to produce a reliable estimate of this cost. In this connection the public librarian now has the support of the central government in that the Department of Education and Science has recognised that the most important aspect of the service is the size, range and up-to-date nature of the book stock provided and it has been prepared to recommend standards that can be used as a guide. To reach an adequate overall standard of provision the Department of Education and Science requires the annual purchase of 250 volumes per thousand of the population served, of which at least 90 volumes should be adult non-fiction works for lending or reference. Authorities are expected to apply either this standard or the following specified minimum basic standard, whichever is the higher. A library can be considered to give a basic service if it buys annually at least 7,200 volumes, including 2,300 separate adult non-fiction titles for lending and reference purposes, not less than 3,000 volumes of adult fiction and 1,500 children's books. In addition a selection of not less than fifty periodicals of general interest should be obtained, with other titles reflecting local needs or interests and at least three major daily papers. These criteria presuppose that a library already has an adequate stock and the librarian making his case for the amount of the book fund for the coming year asks for extra funds to repair past deficiencies and to allow for special needs, such as basic stock for new service points. Information regarding the average cost of books is available from several sources, notably the statistics which appear regularly in the *Bookseller* give average prices and price increases, and there are more detailed statistics made available by the Library Association.

BOOK SELECTION

Having decided on how much money will be required for book purchase and after approval by his committee or controlling authority, the librarian embarks upon the most professional of his functions, the selection of books. It is not the province of this book to consider the theory of this activity, but simply to deal with some of the factors met with in actual practice, which incidentally are often overlooked in theoretical discussion.

Authority to buy books and other material for stock varies considerably in different libraries. In a few, the

library committee still retains complete control over
purchases and the librarian has to supply details of his proposed purchases to it for approval. Nowadays though, it is
common for this professional task to be entrusted to the
chief librarian who may still be asked to report his purchases
to the committee or who may be granted complete freedom
of action. In some libraries a compromise scheme is in
operation and only very expensive or controversial items are
considered by the committee.

The first requirement for any system of book selection is
that the librarians who will be responsible for the management and exploitation of the books purchased should have
a voice in the choosing of their collections. Nothing is easier
or simpler than a centralised book selection system, in which
the chief librarian or a senior member of staff such as a stock
editor buys all the books *par seul*. At the same time no
practice is more certain to result in unrealistic buying and
to strain relations between the central administration and
the departments or branches of the library.

The main reason for introducing a combined operation
for book selection in large libraries is that heads of departments and librarians in charge of branch service points are
in closer contact with shelf stock, the use made of it by
readers and their potential demand. A staff joint committee
is more likely to offset the effects of personal bias or opinion
and can bring a broader outlook to bear on this complex
problem. It should also be noted at this point that completely
independent selection by branch librarians in a public
library system leads to wasteful duplication and also to the
failure to acquire many books which ought to be available
in one branch at least. Similarly university and college
libraries should have a developing acquisitions policy
formulated as the result of close co-operation between library
and academic staff. In the past it was common practice for
these libraries to divide up all, or almost all, of the funds set

aside for books between the various departments of the institution, with the result that book selection was entirely in the hands of the academic staff and no co-ordinated book buying policy was possible. With the greatly-increased book funds of recent years, the acquisitions departments in university libraries have been expanded and taken on additional tasks, and in colleges the librarian has in the same way taken a more significant place in book selection procedure. Academic and teaching staff rely on librarians to give them information on new books published in their fields and there is an increasing tendency for librarians to have the authority to order immediately on publication, or prior to publication, all those books which are evidently works of scholarship, only consulting academic staff on works of dubious value, very expensive or of marginal interest to the studies pursued.

Every library has its own book selection routine, and a student will discover that the system being used in each library he explores will exhibit novelties and variations which he has not met before. There is no mystery about this; librarians are often inventive people and they have a chance to satisfy this urge where such a personal matter as book selection is concerned.

Personal choice is the key to the understanding of this problem. However much we discuss theory or formulate rules for book selection, in the end personal opinion is the over-riding factor. In libraries with several departments and branches, it is necessary to set up a central section with responsibility for the direction of book acquisition. Its function is to ensure that the decisions taken by librarians in departments and branches are based on informed opinion, by providing publishers' catalogues, book lists, and bibliographies, and by arranging regular meetings at which these librarians pool their knowledge and experience. In this way their decisions, while ultimately personal, are made against a background of generally accepted opinion and information.

At such a book selection meeting, copies of recently published books are displayed and ample time is given before discussion takes place for those present to browse through the books. Many librarians make an arrangement with booksellers to be sent approval copies of particular categories of books, for example, all books on a certain subject, all those published within a given price from certain publishing houses, or every book reviewed in selected journals. In these cases the librarian is of course fairly certain that he will in fact purchase most of the titles submitted for his approval. The discussion following examination of the approval books is somewhat akin to a publisher's editorial conference. Some books will be accepted for acquisition without much comment, some will be rejected with the same general agreement, while the merits and demerits of others will be the subject of keen debate before a decision is made. In some cases no general agreement will be reached, but if everyone has the opportunity to contribute his share of experience, the final decision will be as responsible as is possible.

ORDER RECORDS

Although responsibility for book selection may be decentralised, the clerical work involved in placing orders is usually centralised. Order methods will vary according to the type of library and the material purchased, but common to all methods is some form of record which is filed by the library until the books are received. The simplest and most efficient record of an order is made on a card 5 by 3 inches, which gives details of author, title, publisher, price, bookseller, and the number of copies required, together with an indication of the departments or branches to which copies of the book are to be allocated on delivery. A file of these cards gives in a convenient way all the information necessary to check invoices and consignments of books as they arrive. If at the same time as the library order record is made, a similar card or slip is produced, recording the same information, with a pre-printed instruction 'please supply the above book(s) to . . . library' an efficient and convenient order system will be the result. Continuous tear off stationery which produces in one operation an order slip to the bookseller, and a carbon copy for the librarian's file is a most sensible method to use and such a system is in operation in many libraries.

In the future the use of a high speed electronic computer and the automation of the order system will bring considerable advantages to the larger libraries, for the process of ordering a book or document is perhaps the library operation that most nearly approximates to the standard activities of a computer installation. In most libraries, the main file of books on order is usually a single file on cards. If it is arranged in author order, it is difficult to check overdue orders; if it is arranged by date, one needs an index to consult it. Attention may be drawn to overdue orders by the use of a system of coloured 'signals' attached to the order cards, or by using edge-punched cards with needle-sorting at intervals. In a computer system a periodic print-out of the entire file can be obtained in any required order. The information given would include the date when the book was ordered, the name of the supplier, the publisher, cost and reports from the supplier. A print-out of all overdue orders would become a simple machine operation, as it would be, for example, to ascertain the value of outstanding orders. A computer could also be used to provide information about the pattern of current buying of books; information about how many books are on order, or have been purchased in particular price ranges, from certain publishers, for certain departments, or on individual subjects could be extracted from the computer if it were programmed to produce such information.

One of the most revolutionary innovations which will help in the use of computers for ordering of books is the standard numbering of books, a scheme which commenced in the summer of 1967. The advantage of Standard Book Numbers to the book trade is evident. More and more publishers are using a computer for invoicing and stock control, and wholesalers, library suppliers, and booksellers are also turning to computer methods.

The numbering of books is not a new practice; many publishers already have a book numbering system of their own. What is new is the idea that there shall be a standard system for the whole output of British books, and that each book published in the United Kingdom has a number, unique and non-changeable, which will identify it. The Standard Book Number is printed on the reverse of the title page, on the base of the reverse cover and on the base of the reverse cover of the book jacket. It will also appear in advance announcements, advertisements, publishers' catalogues, and in the weekly issues of the *Bookseller* and of the British National Bibliography and its cumulations. All organisations need a number system in order to use a computer, and instead of a multiplicity of conflicting systems there is to be a single uniform scheme known to all and accessible to all.

ACCESSION METHODS

It is traditional to have some method of recording officially the existence of the books in the library stock, this record usually being termed an accessions register. Books are listed in the order in which they are added to stock, and each volume is also marked with a number corresponding to the order in which they appear in this register. Provision is made to record the details of the accession number, the price, bookseller or other source, department or branch to which each item is disposed, and the dates of addition to stock, binding and withdrawal. Bibliographical details are reduced to a minimum. At one time, great importance was attached to the accessions register; it was often kept in massive leather-bound ledgers, each entry being written out by hand in fine copper plate script, and it was widely used for the analysis of statistics relating to expenditure in each main class or by departments. Such registers are still maintained in one or two libraries, but the majority have modified this routine in the interests of efficiency, which requires that clerical processes be reduced as far as possible, and in some libraries it has been decided that the accessions register can be abolished altogether. Perhaps the simplest, certainly one of the most convenient methods now in use is a file of invoices, or copies of invoices, arranged in the order in which they were dealt with, each bearing a record of stock numbers allotted to the books listed on it. To facilitate this practice, booksellers are sometimes prepared to record accession numbers on their invoices and on the books supplied.

The logical development of this method, the use of invoices, is the abolition of even this file and the substitution of a record of invoice details and accession numbers used. Neither of these methods, however, makes it possible for statistical analysis to be obtained from the accessions record and if this is to be done, then it must be carried out independently, either by hand, or by punched card. In the latter case the punched cards can be discarded once the required statistical detail and tabulations have been extracted.

Another modification of the running number system is one whereby a separate sequence of numbers is kept for each main class (prefixed by a letter), the numbers being used again when books are withdrawn. This method is only practicable in small libraries and its main purpose is to help in stock-taking, but since books cannot be assembled in invoice order, the link between accession number and invoice cannot be maintained and must be provided in some other way.

Punch card systems have been applied to library routines to produce yet another form of accession register. In the libraries where this method has been adopted, the actual punch card is used as the stock record. The cards are numbered and kept in numerical order, each card containing written details of author and title and such other information as is required for statistical purposes in coded form. A punching machine makes small holes in the cards corresponding by their position to the figures that have to be encoded. It is then possible by mechanical means to sort cards into numerical order, to make tabulations showing expenditure by classes or by any desired analysis.

Whichever system of accessions register is used, it can be argued that even the most convenient record is more trouble than it is worth. Is the accessions register actually used to much purpose? In some libraries the accession number has served to associate a book with the entry in the catalogue or shelf register and to distinguish between multiple copies of a title. This was useful in connection with the Browne charging system. The primary use of an accessions register, however, has been to provide a link between a bookseller's invoice and a particular copy of a book, in order to satisfy an auditor that a book purchased has in fact been added to stock. Since auditors tend to work from records maintained by a treasurer's or accounts department, and as they are only concerned with expenditure incurred within recent years, it is sound economy to dispense with a *permanent* accessions register maintained in the library. A library can

F

function efficiently and satisfy auditor's enquiries if it maintains a file which records only those adult non-fiction volumes added to stock during the past three financial years which have also now been withdrawn. The number of such books is very small, and a file of the catalogue or book cards for the discarded volumes kept in accession number order is quite satisfactory. Incidentally, in public libraries an accessions register of adult fiction and children's books is quite superfluous because auditors are prepared to accept that as such books have only a limited life, the cost of its compilation and maintenance is unjustifiable.

MAINTENANCE OF STOCK

Although the purchase of current books is probably the most important and the largest aspect of a library's intake, all libraries need to acquire material printed or written in the past – runs of periodicals, older books including rare and valuable printed books, manuscripts and archives. To obtain these a librarian has to peruse booksellers' catalogues and auction catalogues, and he must be fully conversant with the trends of the second-hand book market and particularly of current prices. Equally important, especially in the case of public libraries, is stock revision and the buying of duplicate and replacement copies of books which have been in print for a number of years.

The concept of 'saturation buying' may be considered at this point. The Concise Oxford dictionary definition of the verb to saturate as 'to impregnate, to soak thoroughly, or to overwhelm with concentrated bombing' have nothing to do with the word as used by librarians. When a librarian talks of 'saturation' in relation to buying books, he is borrowing an idea from the chemist, who uses the word to mean 'absorbing the greatest amount possible'.

An important aspect of book buying policy is this degree of saturation, or the total number of copies in stock of a particular title. The answer to this question is an important step towards a realistic book stock, adequate to the demand made upon it.

To take the provision of fiction as an example, there are certain authors whose novels are in constant demand with the result that there are seldom copies available on the shelves. Copies are not there because supply is not being related to demand. We are not talking here of what is generally known as light reading or category fiction but of those authors whose works, because of their reputation and standard, should always be represented 'on the shelves', i.e. whenever the reader looks.

To a person looking for a book by D. H. Lawrence, for example, and unable to find a copy on the shelf, the fact that the catalogue shows that there are 5, 55 or 105 copies in stock is no consolation. He wants satisfaction now. If the library had bought enough copies to 'absorb the greatest amount possible', there would be some titles immediately available, even if there were 2, 22 or 202 other copies on loan.

The example chosen illustrates the principle involved in saturation buying, namely to buy and go on buying as many copies of a title as you can afford, so long as no copies remain unread on the shelves. The ideal of one copy, and only one always available, no matter how many other copies may be on loan is perhaps impossible to reach and it may even be undesirable. There is a certain amount to be said for the theory that a solid and unchanging array of the complete works of D. H. Lawrence would discourage rather than tempt some readers, but it would be generally agreed that some of the titles of a standard author's works ought to be there every time, though the particular titles will be constantly changing.

The same principles can be operated with books on certain

subjects and to follow the practice of buying only the new titles on a subject leads to an unbalanced stock. Due consideration must always be given to the actual needs of the library, avoiding on the one hand over representation due to a flood of new books on a subject, and on the other hand of under representation simply because no new book has recently appeared, although an older, still useful work now worn out and discarded has not been replaced even though it is still in print.

In order to maintain stock at an adequate level a constant and thorough process of stock revision must be undertaken by librarians of departments and branches. This entails a study of the physical condition of the books and relying on the theoretical picture provided by catalogue records. In all matters connected with stock maintenance there is no substitute for actual knowledge of what is going on, acquired through experience in bringing books and readers together.

6

The Departments of Libraries

In the words of the examination syllabus, this chapter is concerned with the 'administration and facilities of, and admission to, the departments of libraries'. Who can use libraries and their services? Under what conditions? What are the services that are available? These are the questions to be answered.

In Britain, the NATIONAL libraries arc independent entities and are virtually great book collections that can be used only for reference. Thus it is possible for the books in the Department of Printed Books of the British Museum to be consulted on the premises by holders of Readers' Tickets granted on application to the Director, or by persons who obtain a special day ticket. Borrowing is not allowed under any circumstances, though, subject to copyright, photocopies of material can be purchased. The conditions are only very slightly different in the National Library of Scotland, where members of the public are admitted to the Reading Room for purposes of reference and research and books are very exceptionally lent to other libraries of similar standing and to government departments in Edinburgh. It is sometimes argued that it is wrong to restrict the use of national libraries to advanced researchers on the grounds that most of the community, those who pay taxes, contribute the most substantial portion of the money that is needed for their development and maintenance and that therefore there should be unrestricted right of entry to all comers; but the facilities are not such as appeal to the uneducated or unacademic reader and being essentially libraries for scholars it is generally accepted that limited access to *bona fide* students is a practical necessity, if only to contain the demand for the limited number of reading places.

The functions of and the services provided by national libraries vary according to local circumstances and it is more difficult to summarise those in Britain than in other countries, if only because of the large number of them. Most countries have only one national library which serves as the permanent depository for all publications issued in a country. This is usually achieved by means of a copyright law which enables a library to obtain free of all charges all printed books and periodicals, manuscripts, music, maps and prints. It is also normal for national libraries to a smaller or greater extent to collect foreign literature, but they must be selective towards certain subjects. It would be physically impossible for national libraries to be all-embracing universal libraries and they must be selective towards certain subjects; the Library of Congress, for example, does not collect medicine and agriculture.

Many foreign national libraries have much wider functions than the national libraries in Britain, where they do not belong to the national interlending system. The fact that they have a largely reference function has led to the development for lending and interlending purposes of the National Lending Library for Science and Technology and the National Central Library. In other countries, particularly the smaller and developing, the national library is seen as the pivot of the entire library system, taking the lead in all interlending co-operation, producing the basic bibliography, functioning as the training centre for librarians. In Scandinavia only old books and rare books are for consultation in reading rooms; the vast majority of books are available for loan, particularly through other libraries in the country.

What and how are the services provided by the national libraries in Britain? The practice has been for departmentalisation and specialisation to be according to the physical form of the material collected rather than by subject. The National Libraries of Wales and Scotland have Map Rooms and Music Rooms and the British Museum in this respect has the four Departments of Printed Books, Manuscripts, Oriental Printed Books and Manuscripts, and Prints and Drawings, while the library of the British Museum (Natural History) consists of a General Library and five sections corresponding to the Departments of Zoology, Entomology, Palaeontology, Botany and Mineralogy. These Departmental sections contain books and serial publications which treat exclusively of the particular branch of the subject with which the department in question is concerned. In the General Library, however, are found works on general biology and natural history, travel, biography, topography and general scientific works.

The British national libraries have always seen it to be among their necessary duties to compile and publish catalogues, to arrange exhibitions and to provide photographic reproductions and other illustrative material for sale. In this connection the British Museum is of supreme importance with its General Catalogue of Printed Books, its Subject Index issued in five-yearly volumes, its special catalogues of maps, music, orientalia, etc. and its list of accessions issued monthly.

UNIVERSITY AND ACADEMIC LIBRARIES provide a service to meet the needs of two main types of readers, the undergraduate and the research worker; the latter may be a member of the academic staff or a postgraduate student who is preparing for a further degree. The University Library at Cambridge and the Bodleian at Oxford are primarily reference libraries and may be used by undergraduates, graduate students and senior members of the university. Apart from the facility whereby books from the Bodleian can be placed on deposit in departmental libraries within the university, certain categories of Bodleian books may be borrowed through the National Central Library. At Oxford and Cambridge it is the function of the faculty and college libraries to provide lending libraries and of course, these libraries are accessible normally only to their own members. The Scottish and modern English universities allow books to be borrowed much more freely although a number of reference works will be retained for consultation in the library only. This is the practice followed in the libraries in other educational establishments, namely schools and colleges of all sorts. In a few instances where books are not lent freely to all students and pupils, this is largely due to inadequate stocks.

Academic libraries, including those in universities, usually open their doors to members of other similar institutions and sometimes to members of the general public with the special permission of the librarian. As these institutions have grown so enormously in recent years, it has proved impossible for a satisfactory service to be given from just one main library. In universities the establishment of libraries for Faculties or groups of subjects has been increasingly favoured and the movement towards decentralisation has been counteracted by siting the main library in the centre of the university and providing several rooms arranged by School or Faculty. Nevertheless the increasing size of university campuses with a number of detached units located a considerable distance away from the main site has made the creation of departmental libraries inevitable, though it has been vital to ensure that these libraries do not become separate operational units, but that all library staff were university library staff, that the university librarian acted as 'chief' librarian and that these 'branch' libraries enjoyed all the benefit of a central administrative and technical service agency.

A SPECIAL LIBRARY is a unit devoted to the information requirements of a specific organisation or firm and its prime obligation is to the members of the institution of which it forms a part. Therefore every special library is unique according to the demands and interests of its personnel. It also follows that it is the responsibility of each special librarian to collect the books and other material required for specific groups of users within the membership of the parent body. Access to a special library is limited to members of the organisation; it has a 'closed' clientele and service to outsiders would only be given after a recommendation from the librarian approved by the governing body.

Generally speaking, special libraries are not large enough to be departmentalised and the essential difference between them and other libraries is in the material filed and the techniques used in making information available. In most special libraries periodical literature is of primary importance and may well form the major part of the collection. In addition, reports, standards, specifications and other material issued as separates are filed in considerable quantity. This calls for special techniques connected with the filing and dissemination of information. Above all, the special librarian does not wait for requests from users; he must bring to their notice the existence of information relating to their interests, often by publishing a bulletin of references to current literature; he must anticipate the requirements of his clientele and inform them of accessions to the library without delay. Though all enquiries are gladly received and tenaciously pursued, the special librarian's role is primarily that of a positive producer of relevant information.

The position of all PUBLIC LIBRARY authorities in England and Wales was clarified in Circular 4/65 which was the first communication sent out by the Permanent Under-Secretary of State from the Department of Education and Science immediately before the Public Libraries and Museums Act of 1964 came into force on the 1st April, 1965. In amplification of the duty of library authorities to provide a comprehensive and efficient service, it was pointed out that they have a duty to allow access to their libraries to all comers, but that their obligation to lend extends only to those who live or work or study full-time in their areas. It was hoped, nevertheless, that library authorities would allow persons outside those categories to borrow from their libraries. Thus it is common practice nowadays for most public libraries to accept the reader's ticket of any other library. This is extremely important because it enables a person to use the library which is most convenient for him wherever he lives, works or happens to be in temporary residence or on holiday. And this is often more than a matter of convenience, for it enables public librarians to overcome the difficulties and often the absurdities of local government boundaries.

The 1964 Act also prohibits charges for lending books and similar material to those who reside, work or study full-time in the area, i.e. to those persons who become members in their own right. It is therefore implicit that other persons, i.e. those who live outside its area, may be charged a subscription to obtain membership. Nevertheless although a library authority gives a 'free' book lending service to its own people, it may charge anyone for borrowing gramophone records and the like. Charges are also authorised for notifying a reader of a reservation, for failure to return articles by a given date, for supplying book catalogues and other bibliographical material, for admission to meetings and exhibitions, the showing of films and slides, musical performances and other events of an educational or cultural nature and for the provision of special facilities such as a block loan of books to a pre-school play group or a prison.

In Scotland and Northern Ireland the legal position is similar though not so specific. Libraries must be open to the public free of charge and no charge may be made for borrowing books. The only exception is the City of Belfast whose Corporation by a private act of 1961 is empowered to operate a service similar to those provided under the English 1964 Act.

The services provided and the departmental organisation of public libraries are described in detail in many other works and very adequately in two books by K. C. Harrison, *Public libraries today* and *The library and the community*. This paragraph attempts to describe the pattern that has evolved. It merely indicates to a student the various aspects which he must study in depth. Public libraries can conveniently be divided into municipal and county authorities and the populations served by the former range from Cockermouth Urban District (6,140) to the county boroughs of Coventry (333,000), Leeds (712,040) or Birmingham (1,102,660), while the latter include the counties of Cumberland (162,390), Nottinghamshire (390,830), Essex (832,850) and the West Riding of Yorkshire (1,061,730). The range and organisation of the service to such widely different sized communities naturally reveals infinite variety, but all are divided into the lending and reference functions. The most popular function of the public library is the lending service of instructional and recreational reading to adults and children, catering for a large variety of tastes and for differing levels of requirements. Yet though buildings are well designed, attractive, inviting and functionally adequate, they can still make a daunting prospect for uninitiated readers and it is part of the duty of public library authorities to provide bibliographical guidance and assistance to readers, a task for senior professional staff. Many libraries have taken seriously the requirement which is included in the England and Wales 1964 Act that they should 'encourage both adults and children to make full use of the library services' and they may arrange various activities – lectures, exhibitions, discussion and play-reading groups, record recitals and, for children, story hours and book clubs – which draw attention to books as sources of information, stimulation and enrichment.

The great bulk of books are borrowed by readers who visit the libraries but special efforts are often made to give the best possible service to citizens who are handicapped – the housebound, the hospital patients, the residents of old people's homes and prisoners – and by mobile libraries to those who live in remote parts of cities and rural areas of counties.

The public library's reference function as the provider of information is too little recognised. Smaller libraries have collections of quick-reference books which give up-to-date information and the larger reference libraries and the headquarters of county libraries normally offer a wide range of books and allied material including the indexing and abstracting journals that are the keys to information in the many thousands of periodicals which are available through the interlending agencies. While it is generally true to say of the public library that it avoids specialisation and that it stocks such books as may be required by the intelligent citizen, some libraries concentrate on a special subject such as local history or on a particular commercial or industrial interest which may be of importance to their locality. In the larger city libraries can be found extensive reference departments, the raw material of research and special collections. Their staff are skilled in tracking down wanted information, although many people needing their services are not aware of this.

Suggestions for Further Reading

ASHWORTH, Wilfred. *Handbook of special librarianship and information work.* Aslib. 3rd ed. 1967.

BURKETT, J., *ed. Special library and information services in the United Kingdom.* Library Association. 2nd ed. 1965.

CALDWELL, W. *An introduction to county library practice.* A.A.L. 2nd ed. 1964.

CORBETT, E. V. *An introduction to librarianship.* Clarke. 2nd ed. 1966.

CORBETT, E. V. *The public library and its control.* A.A.L. 2nd ed. 1966.

CORBETT, E. V. *Public library finance and accountancy.* Library Association. 1960.

CURRIE, Clifford. *Prospects in librarianship.* Crosby Lockwood. 2nd ed. 1963.

DAVINSON, Donald. *Academic and legal deposit libraries.* Bingley. 1965.

DAVIS, Peter and GODDARD, Julie. *Library staffs: today and tomorrow.* A.A.L. 1966.

FURLONG, Norman. *Library practice for colleges of education.* Library Association. 1966.

GARDNER, Frank M. *Letters to a younger librarian.* Clarke. 1951.

GREAT BRITAIN. Government of Northern Ireland. *The*

public library service in Northern Ireland. (Hawnt Report). H.M.S.O. 1966.

GREAT BRITAIN. H.M. Treasury. Organisation and Methods Division. *A guide to government libraries.* H.M.S.O. 2nd ed. 1958.

GREAT BRITAIN. Ministry of Education. *Standards of public library service in England and Wales.* H.M.S.O. 1962.

GREAT BRITAIN. Ministry of Education. *The structure of the public library service in England and Wales.* (Roberts Report). H.M.S.O. 1959.

GREAT BRITAIN. Ministry of Housing and Local Government. *Staffing of local government:* report of the (Mallaby) Committee. H.M.S.O. 1967.

GREAT BRITAIN. Scottish Education Department. *Libraries, museums and art galleries:* a report of the Advisory Council on Education in Scotland. H.M.S.O. 1951.

GREAT BRITAIN. University Grants Committee. *Report of the (Parry) Committee on libraries.* H.M.S.O. 1967.

HARRISON, K. C. *First steps in librarianship.* Deutsch. 2nd ed. 1962.

HARRISON, K. C. *The library and the community.* Deutsch. 2nd ed. 1966.

HARRISON, K. C. *Public libraries today.* Crosby Lockwood. 1963.

HEINTZE, Ingeborg. *The organization of the small public library.* UNESCO. 1963.

HEWITT, A. R. *A summary of public library law.* A.A.L. 4th ed. 1965.

HOGG, F. N., *and others. A report on a survey made of book charging systems at present in use in England.* Library Association. 1962.

IRWIN, Raymond and STAVELEY, Ronald, *eds. The libraries of London.* Library Association. 2nd ed. 1961.

JEFFERSON, George. *Public library administration.* Bingley. 1965.

LANDAU, Thomas, *ed. Encyclopaedia of librarianship*. Bowes. 3rd ed. 1966.

LOCK, R. N. *James Duff Brown's manual of library economy*. Grafton. 7th ed. 1961.

LOCK, R. N. *Library administration*. Crosby Lockwood. 1961. *Professional and non-professional duties in libraries*. Library Association. 1962.

SEWELL, P. H. *ed. Five years' work in librarianship 1951–1955*. Library Association. 1958.

SEWELL, P. H., *ed. Five years' work in librarianship 1956–1960*. Library Association. 1963.

(The Shackleton) *Report of the Committee on university libraries*. University of Oxford. 1966.

WHEELER, Joseph L. *and* GOLDHOR, Herbert. *Practical administration of public libraries*. New York, Harper & Row. 1962.

Appendix

Students should be thoroughly aware of the nature of the questions set in this part of the professional examinations of the Library Association. Regular inspection of past examination papers throughout the period of study is a valuable indication of the scope of the syllabus, and for this reason the papers set since the inception of the examination have been gathered together here.

June 1964

1. A library is often controlled through a committee or committees. What is the purpose of each such committee and what is the relationship of the Librarian to the committee/s?

2. Give a general account of the ways in which the central government plays a part in the control and finance of some kinds of libraries. Refer to the libraries or types of library you have in mind.

3. Describe briefly and compare the methods by which public and university libraries obtain their finances for regular and capital expenditure.

4. What categories of readers are normally permitted to use the facilities of national, public, academic and special libraries respectively? In what circumstances are exceptions likely to be made?

5. Do you think that in-service training will be necessary for library staff who will in future be recruited direct from library school without previous library employment? Briefly describe the kind of training you would advocate.

6. To what extent do you consider a librarian should delegate responsibility to individual members of his staff and what methods might he employ to co-ordinate the work of all departments and all officers?

7. What are the advantages of dividing junior staff into two categories: (a) library assistants accepted as professional trainees, and (b) general library assistants? What pre-entry qualifications would you expect of EACH category and how would you divide the duties between them?

8. What records are required for the bookstock and periodicals acquired by a library from the initial selection until withdrawal? State the type of library you have in mind and show the purpose of each record.

9. Why is it important to ensure that the stock of books and periodicals of a library is kept up to date, adequate to demand, and in good condition? What methods would you employ to ensure that this is achieved?

10. Describe FOUR distinctly different publications which you think would be suitable for a library to compile and issue to its readers. What purpose would EACH be intended to serve?

G

December 1964

1. Show, with named examples in EACH case, the different types of library embraced by the term 'special library'. In EACH instance indicate the authority or controlling body responsible for its provision. (Exclude special departments of public libraries.)

2. Estimates are commonly employed in the financing of a library service. Show the various purposes they may serve and list any FOUR major items you would expect to be included in annual estimates.

3. Public libraries, university libraries and certain special libraries are controlled through one or more committees. One of these is a Libraries Committee or Libraries Sub-Committee. Show its purpose and normal functions and list, with brief explanatory notes, SIX items which might appear on a typical agenda.

4. What do you understand by the term 'staff manual'? What are the advantages and disadvantages of employing such a manual?

5. The satisfactory administration of a library depends largely upon adequate means of communication between the Librarian and all members of his staff. Describe, with reasons, the methods (other than the use of a staff manual) you would employ to ensure that staff at all levels are kept adequately informed of matters affecting the library service, their responsibilities, and their conditions of service.

6. Briefly describe the problems involved and methods employed in the purchase, receipt and distribution of a large

collection of periodicals. Indicate the type of library you have in mind.

7. What improvements in the public library service in England and Wales would you expect ultimately to result from the new Public Libraries Act? (A recapitulation of the clauses of the Act is not required.)

8. Every kind of library finds it necessary to help readers to understand the arrangement of the library and to make known its many resources and facilities. Describe the methods you would employ to provide such assistance and the value of each in the context of (a) a large library, or (b) a university library, or (c) a public library.

9. It is common practice for libraries to have a 'stack room' (or rooms) in which certain material is kept. Show the purpose of such a stack room and the circumstances under which you would permit readers to have direct access to it. Illustrate your answer by reference to different types of library.

10. Show how the size and type of library may affect the choice of a 'charging or issue method' used for recording the loan of books to individual readers for homereading.

June 1965

1. Define the term 'co-option' as applied to membership of a Library Committee. Show the purpose of this practice and indicate the kinds of library authority most likely to have co-opted members.

2. To what extent do decisions on library administration, policy and finance rest with the Chief Librarian and to

what extent is he controlled by higher authority? Show how procedure and practice may vary in different types of library.

3. Library income and expenditure are both normally subject to some form of audit. Why should this be necessary and what steps would you recommend to ensure that all such income and expenditure is adequately accounted for and controlled?

4. Most libraries find it necessary to have some code of regulations and/or bye-laws to govern admission to the library and the use of its facilities. Demonstrate why this is necessary and the various purposes served by such regulations and bye-laws. Illustrate your answer by the use of examples.

5. In any large library or library system there will be a member of staff whose responsibility is 'personnel management'. Show the range of such responsibilities and the various duties devolving on the officer concerned.

6. Show what information you would include in a comprehensive staff record of officers and employees used for administrative purposes in a large library. Explain carefully, with examples, the usefulness of each item of information recorded.

7. Describe the main purposes of an annual report of a library. Indicate the type of material it would include and show how the type of library will affect the contents of the report.

8. How can the British National Bibliography and its various services be employed to facilitate various aspects of library administration? Indicate any shortcomings of B.N.B. in this respect.

9. What do you understand by the term 'subject depart-ments'? What are the advantages and disadvantages of arranging a library in this way? Describe briefly any well-known library you know that employs this method.

10. What administrative methods do different types of library employ to ensure that adequate means exist for (a) suggesting books, and (b) reserving books not immediately available? What are the advantages and disadvantages of providing these facilities?

December 1965

1. Paragraph 2 of the Public Libraries and Museums Act 1964 provides for the establishment of two library Advisory Councils 'to advise the Secretary of State upon such matters connected with the provision or use of library facilities . . . as they think fit, and upon any questions referred to them by him . . . ' In general terms state what you envisage the duties of the Councils might be and give examples of problems upon which they might be called to offer advice.

2. In broad terms explain the relationship which exists between the central government and the various authorities responsible for different kinds of libraries in England and Wales. You may present your answer in tabulated form if you wish.

3. Show how the efficiency and success of a large library service depend upon the managerial and executive ability of the Chief Librarian.

4. What are the main factors likely to be responsible for increases in a library's annual estimates for (a) books and

allied materials, (b) staff, (c) wages, (d) equipment, and (e) heating, lighting and cleaning? Prepare notes for the Chairman of the library committee justifying such increases.

5. What means would you suggest might be employed, both nationally and locally, to aid recruitment to librarianship at both professional and non-professional levels?

6. Staff meetings of various kinds are frequently used in library administration. Describe the type of meetings you would advocate and show the benefits that may be derived from them.

7. In what circumstances do you consider it justifiable for a librarian to make certain items, or sections, of the library stock, available on application only? The answer should be written in the context of libraries generally and the term 'stock' interpreted in the broadest sense.

8. In what circumstances do you consider library stock-taking to be practicable? What are its advantages and disadvantages?

9. Why has there been so much professional interest in recent years in the possible use of mechanical equipment to facilitate, or replace, library routines? Give TWO examples of the application of such equipment and its advantages.

10. What factors would you have to consider in deciding on a charging system to be used for the issue of books for home reading from (a) a large University library; (b) a municipal or county branch library, serving over 30,000 population, and (c) the library of a small professional association? What particular system might you recommend for EACH?

June 1966

1. Define the term 'library authority' in relation to a public library. What are the equivalent authorities for (a) a university library, and (b) an industrial library? Compare the way in which the three kinds of authorities exercise control over the libraries which they are responsible for providing.

2. Show how, in most types of library, the service provided, and the work of the Chief Librarian, are largely influenced by annual estimates of expenditure. Illustrate your answer fully with examples.

3. A number of recent committee reports have recommended that the number of specialist posts in libraries should be increased. Why do you think additional specialist posts are required in libraries and for what purposes? Describe thoroughly the work involved in any ONE such post.

4. Explain why it is desirable that a Chief Librarian should be a capable speaker and also be able to express himself clearly in writing. The answer should be well illustrated with examples of the use made of these qualifications.

5. Why is an efficient system of staff control essential in the administration of a large library? As Chief Librarian of such a system what methods would you employ to ensure such efficiency?

6. What measures would you take to ensure the general welfare and interest of the junior members of the staff of a large library?

7. What statistical evidence, both general and local, do you consider a Chief Librarian can usefully employ in the

various reports he is called upon to produce, from time to time, for his employing authority? Show to what purpose such statistics would be used.

8. Libraries frequently use an accession number as an integral part of their library records and routines. Show the advantages of this practice and the various purposes this accession number may serve.

9. What are the various reasons for providing microtext material in libraries? What administrative arrangements would be necessary for the storage and use of the different kinds of material?

10. Compare any TWO of the following types of book-charging system: (a) Browne, (b) photocharging, (c) Bookamatic.

November 1966

1. What significant effects would you expect the 'Public Libraries and Museums Act, 1964' to have on all types of library?

2. Compare the relationships of a Chief Librarian of a large public library and those of the Librarian of a large industrial library, with their controlling authorities.

3. To what extent should the Chief Librarian of a large library, employing 150 or more staff, have *direct* contact and communication with both senior and junior members of his staff? Show how this could be achieved.

4. Why is it essential that a Librarian should be able to prepare well-constructed reports? Give with reasons FOUR

examples of occasions when such reports might be necessary and show in EACH case to whom the particular report would be presented.

5. What basic differences are there between the methods of financing and controlling expenditure in public, national, university and industrial libraries?

6. State the arguments for and against the arrangement of a library's stock and services by subject departments, giving examples of libraries arranged in this way.

7. Give examples of possible applications of computers to library administration. Why is there so much current interest in these possibilities?

8. Many libraries have book storage problems. Outline the various ways, both co-operative and individual, in which economy in storage may be achieved. What special shelving or other equipment would be useful in this connection?

9. What records is it necessary for a library to keep in respect of the selection, ordering and receipt of books? Describe each of these records and show the purpose of each.

10. What methods would you employ to inform library users and non-users of the facilities offered by the library, of conditions of use, new developments, acquisitions, and other topics of general interest? State the type of library you have in mind.

June 1967

1. In what types of library would you expect control and policy-making to be vested in a Library Committee? What

essential differences are there in the establishment of such committees and their duties in different types of library?

2. What provisions of the Public Libraries and Museums Act, 1964, authorise local authorities to levy charges, and on whom? To what extent do you consider this legislation to be satisfactory?

3. Prepare a report to a Library Committee, advocating the production of a comprehensive printed guide to the library's facilities, for free distribution to individual users of that library.

4. Compare the respective responsibilities of the librarian of a *university* library, a *municipal* library, and an *industrial* library, with regard to the preparation of estimates of income and expenditure. Show the various stages through which the estimates pass in EACH instance before funds are made available.

5. What is the value of exchanging staff with, or seconding staff to, other libraries at home and abroad? Discuss the difficulties and problems involved in such arrangements.

6. Discuss the advantages and disadvantages (in all types of library) associated with a system of recruiting junior staff with a promise of admission to Library School in due course, on leave of absence with full pay.

7. What are the advantages and disadvantages of organising a library stock and services completely on a subject department basis? State the type of library you have in mind.

8. Outline the methods usually employed by different types of library to prevent the abuse of facilities and services

provided, as well as library property and material. Give adequate examples throughout.

9. What are the advantages and disadvantages of a library establishing its own home bindery? State the type of library you have in mind.

10. What administrative advantages might be obtained by using computer-produced book catalogues in place of card catalogues in a large library system? Mention any disadvantages which would have to be considered in this connection.

Index

109

Local authorities, 38, 40

Maintenance of stock, 82–4
Management, 27–35
Management services, 34–5
Ministry of Housing and Local Government, 39, 40, 41

National Central Library, 13, 86, 88
National Lending Library for Science and Technology, 13, 14, 86
National libraries, 12–14, 85–7
National Library of Scotland, 12, 85, 87
National Library of Wales, 12–13, 87
National Reference Library of Science and Invention, 13
Non-professional staff, 64, 66, 67–8, 70

Order records, 77–9
Oxford university libraries, 15–16

Part-time staff, 64, 66–7, 70
Personnel management, 51–3
Professional societies, 18–19
Public libraries, 20–6, 39, 40, 47, 52, 54, 59, 82, 90–2
Public Libraries and Museums Act of 1964, 21–5, 90–1, 92
Public library authorities, 22–3

Rate Support Grant Order for 1966, 39
Rates, 38, 39
Recruitment, 68–70

Saturation buying, 82–3
School libraries, 17, 88
Science Museum, 13
Scotland, 25, 91
Select Committee on Estimates, 37, 38
Select Committee on Public Accounts, 37
Special libraries, 17–20, 49, 68, 89–90
Staff establishments, 52, 54–63
Staffing, 51–70
Standard Book Numbers, 79
Stock control, 71–84
Sunderland, 55
Swindon, 21

Tickhill, 21
Trainee librarians, 64–5, 69–70
Treasury, 18, 36, 37, 49

University Grants Committee, 14, 49
University libraries, 14–16, 49, 59, 60, 61, 75–6, 87–9

Victoria and Albert Museum, 13